PA'LANTE A LA LUZ (Charge Into The Light):
The Alternative New Year's Day Spoken Word / Performance Extravaganza
- 2018 Anthology

- First Edition.
- Volume V in a series.
- 168 pages.
- Trade Paperback.
- American contemporary poetry anthology.

Contact Information / Order Online:
http://www.alternativenyd.org/

Rogue Scholars Press
http://www.roguescholars.com

Design and Layout: C. D. Johnson
Publishers: Rogue Scholars Press

ISBN-10: 0-9840982-5-9
ISBN-13: 978-0-9840982-5-5

Published by Rogue Scholars Press
New York, NY - USA

Palante A La Luz

Charge Into The Light

**The Alternative
New Year's Day
Spoken Word / Performance
Extravaganza!**

2018 Anthology

http://alternativenyd.org

CONTENTS

CONTENTS Continued

CONTENTS Continued

APPENDIX

This anthology celebrates the multitude of writers that make up the **24th annual Alternative New Year's Day Spoken Word / Performance Extravaganza**, which has been held for the past four years at the legendary **Nuyorican Poets Cafe** in the East Village.

I want to thank the staff of the Alternative for helping to make this event possible; **Madeline Artenberg, Lydia Cortes, Pete Dolack, C. D. Johnson, Ptr Kozlowski, Ellen Aug Lytle, Su Polo, Robert Roth, Thad Rutkowski, Lydia Cortes**, and Joanne Pagano Weber — and our assistant editors this year, **Merissa Anderson** and **Alejandra Moreno**, both of whom also contributed to the anthology.

Each person has played a valuable part in putting the pieces of this ten hour long event together. I want to single out C. D. Johnson for creating our annual anthology, a "new" piece added to the mix of the event in 2014. When this event began on January 1st, 1995 I dreamed of their being an annual book containing samplings of the work of the writers who performed at the Alternative. What a wonderful takeaway!

I Austin Alexis

The Streets

A neighborhood so gentrified
the fireflies have moved back.
No more gunshots on Saturday nights.
No more POW competing with a dog's bark.
Even the skywriters cruising the blue
two miles above this urban geography
notice the difference, toast the change.

Dragonflies sniff between a fire hydrant
and a newly painted wrought iron gate, flutter
amongbn SUVs, Hondas and vaseline-shiny Fords.
Residents high five each other.
"No, man, it's not my fault," they say
when a homeless person shuffles by,
his eyes more glaring than the sun.

I Joel Allegretti

Memphis Minnie's Unmarked Grave

> *I might tell everybody what that Chickasaw has done, done for me,*
> *I might tell everybody what that Chickasaw has done, done for me,*
> *She done stole my man away and blowed that doggone smoke on me,*
> *She's a low-down dirty dog.*
>
> Memphis Minnie,
> "Chickasaw Train Blues (Low Down Dirty Thing)"

Lizzie Douglas sang. Yes, she did. She didn't train out of here on the Chickasaw caboose. No, a stroke robbed her nursing-home pillow in 1973. A synonym for stroke is brain attack. "When brain cells die during a stroke, abilities controlled by that area of the brain are lost. How a stroke patient is affected depends on where the stroke occurs in the brain and how much the brain is damaged."[1] Lizzie was born in Louisiana and performed for loose change on Memphis streets before the microphone transferred her singing to 78 RPM records. They say she played guitar like a man. Her remains lie in a Baptist cemetery in Mississippi, birthplace of Tennessee Williams. A headstone honored Tennessee's grave right after his burial. Lizzie got hers twenty-three years after her death (she was a Negro, you know), courtesy of Bonnie Raitt. Thank you, Bonnie.

[1] National Stroke Association

❚ Merissa Anderson

Photo: "Bogotá Street Scene", 2009.

I Madeline Artenberg

Afternoon Whispers

Sun's glare
readies for silence
after a long afternoon.
Bells swell, young girls
scatter with time.

I dream colors
as shadows twist
on palettes.
Twilight drifts
toward completion.

I Carmen Bardeguez-Brown

The Wall. La Pared

#1
Monarch butterflies flies south during the winter.
They flapp their wide orange and black abanicos acariciando las rafagas del viento.
What makes them dance all the way to Mexico?
I wonder how building the wall will affect them
Will they dig tiny holes till it crumbles
or stay in Mexico and feel sorry for the people up North?
#2
Most of the aguacate or avocado
that is consumed in the United States comes from Mexico
I guess if they built the wall we will not have any more guacamole or avocado paste
or any aguacate
maldita pared.
#3
So let me get this straight
the United States Declares an illegal war against Mexico
because they just want to expand to the West courtesy of the Monroe Doctrine
They win and take what we call now
Arizona, Colorado, Texas, New Mexico etc etc etc.
one hundred years later some people in the United States
get all huffing and puffin because Mexicans are coming to their old neighborhood.
Well, like my Mexicans friends will say, la chingada.
#4
Suggestions and a few questions about building the wall:

1. Make sure that it is a revolving door just in case Mexicans don't like what they see.
2. Have a scanner that identify the ethnicity and nationality of everyone passing through the door because not everyone is Mexican.
3. Just out of curiosity, who do you think is going to build the wall? Because the last time I check most of the construction workers in the US are Latino immigrants and the majority are illegal, by the way not all of them are Mexicans.
4. And are all of the materials use to build the wall made in the USA.
5. Will the construction company be an American, Chinese or European co?

6. Are the workers be paid minimum wage, will they be in unions, any women?

7. Will the US build a wall somewhere in the Atlantic to stopped Irish, English, Spaniards and any other European people from coming to the United States?

8. Hmm if we could go back in time I wonder if the Africans would have build a gigantic wall to stopped the Euro Americans from stealing their people and sold them into slavery?

9. And what about all of the Native American nations, will they build a wall around Washington DC or Wall Street to stop " white people from intruding in their imposed reservation camps?

10. I wonder how the pilgrims would have felt if they encountered a giant wall instead of the welcoming natives that saved their ass during those harsh winters in the new land.

We don't need to build walls. Like the Beatles said all we need is Love. Y al carajo con la maldita pared.

I Yael Baron

The House Of Viper

Light a candle,
Say a prayer,
Love meets danger,
My heart don't care.
Dance to the beat...
Breathe in that toxic air.
They never got the message
to handle with care.
And in the House of the Viper,
we learn we survive.
By the power of our chosen addiction,
just burn the house down.
There's nothing left to say,
only arguments and Emotion's pain.
Relationship's a stain,
and there's no removing Toxic...No
[One week later at the Hospital]
Yes, I may be Borderline,
but some of you have crossed the line.
Unethical, you generalize,
and then you diagnose,
forgetting that we're people first.
Why do you look at me like I'm some strange case study in your book?
Why do you look at me like I'm some strange case study in your book?
Why do you look at me like I'm some strange case study in your book?
[The Doctor will see you now]
Hi, I'm Doctor Generalization,
and you have Borderline Personality Disorder.
You have no hope.
You have no cure.
Now! Get out of my office!
In the presence of lies, love suffocates and dies.
So much shame attached to my name.
I started to hate me.
Do it... No!...Do it...No!
You heard what she said.

You have no hope.
You have no cure.
In the House of The Viper… (No!)
we learn we survive.
By the power. of "Our" chosen addiction
Just burn the house down.
There's nothing left to say,
only arguments and Emotion's pain.
Relationship's a stain,
and there's no removing Toxic. No!

I Steve Bloom

The Prison Artist

1.
The prison artist works away
in her cell on her latest creation,
intensity identical to any artist
wherever she may be working:
home, studio, even out
      in the open air.

For to the artist it matters not, we know,
where she may find herself in space
so long as the mind is free to wander
among the shapes and the colors.

      (Her brush shifts a line here
      a bit to the left, the tint
      of the area that it borders
      just a hair more
      toward the violet end
      of the spectrum.)

Wherever she finds herself in space:
out in the open air, in a studio, or at home—
but especially when home is
the inside of a prison cell—
every artist, working on her latest
is, you see, painting the gateway
      to freedom.

2.
The prison artist
coats a square of glazed bricks
in the wall of her cell with black paint,
hangs a sign:
"I have painted the gateway to Hell,"
it reads
      "Do not open."

I Peter Bushyeager

Laughing Gas

Dentist's overheads hum
argon tubes throw
throbbing light on
my thrown open mouth the
gas comfort grid
fuzzy on inside
outside implant procedure
strikes me as
wry so happy I
misunderstand and
the misunderstanding grows
an easy stroll
belly thrust out
arms at 90 degrees
as if they ended in
heavy insulated work gloves
rather than hands as
nature wants planets
rocky or gaseous
gaseous here is
my body a small planet with
nature's light
wafting lightly over
inserted titanium and
biblical comfort
folded over everything

I Natalie N. Caro

An Unexamined Institution

(for Miguel Piñero)

We say we never saw the cause.
But we heard the cause,
heard the crying of families losing their homes,
heard the empty promises of politicians,
heard the tractors making room for luxury living,

We were dead on arrival, we never really Lived
died seeking the Cause; died seeking a cause

uptown, downtown, midtown, crosstown
our bodies found all over town
slaving away in windowless offices
interests accruing on student loans

thinking the Cause is 100k plus incomes and louis Vuitton, thinking the Cause is
sellin' our souls to corporations, thinking the cause is to be found in strange beds,
and drinking our nights away into oblivion.

we want a flat screen tvs, want versace, chanel, true religion, we want the Cause
to come up like a follow,
we want, we want, we want to want more wants

but we never give, we don't give love to children
who oceans away make our clothes for pennies a day
we don't give our hearts to old people living menial pensions government
allotted...never do we ever give our souls to our people

our legs were left in afghanistan and iraq, our arms were found in pockets of bank
of amerikkka, our scalps were on Bushes' belt, our blood paints the streets of
washington, our eyes are still looking for salvation, 99% of the nation dies seekin'
a Cause
seekin' the Cause

while the Cause is dyin' seekin' us, we died yesterday,
we are dyin' today, we will be dead tomorrow; died seekin' a Cause; died seekin'
the Cause

I Patricia Carragon

Meltdown

he claims that mercury retrograde
lives inside your monitor
and that your facebook wall
contains secret minefields.
she can argue about how emojis
bring out his inner draconic child
and why his fake news
is feeding the trolls, not his kittens.
the internet circus is not leaving the swamp,
and we are as psychopathic as an orange tweet
infected with the russian flu
that has already consumed our interface.
did you know that you and your option key
will not be covered,
and that you and your computer
will not last for four years?

I María Fernanda Lara Chamorro

From H-Town

The water spreads wider than itself.
The gravel-packed road, the neatly-strung
houses, the entire county wades
in my aunt's throat.
Two weeks ahead of the hurricane, she teased
my uncle about getting rope-burn from his childhood
rosary. She had written me in blue. *I know how this goes.*
The first minute you are laughing and it's your birthday.
You are enjoying fish on a platter that your neighborhood
caught and fried for you. The next, you see the tile
wet and you watch the water crawl, how it do
without a backbone. You do not ask yourself, Where-
is-it-coming-from? Will-my-house-
stand-it? God, if I leave, can-I-come-back?
No. You remember that not even the turn of this
earth could prepare for this.
I try to imagine my aunt telling the story,
saying how she wakes to the county gulping itself.
She stretches her arms as far as she could, say
she is the sun and its sea, say every wooden
beam, every home is hauled like this.
She skips the dance of drowning. If she doesn't,
she would say that her eyes roll back,
that she wants to see herself before the ocean.

I Tina Chan

Color The World

Color the dark stormy sky with hope
Color the day and night with new memories
Color your life with new adventures
Color the world around you with goals
Color the pages of a journal with plans
Color today with productive actions
Color tomorrow with dreams
Color yesterday's sorrows and grief with lessons learned
Smile, the world is full of hope
Convert monochrome to color the people surrounding you
The passage of correctness
You are too consume of what is right
Too blind to see the truth
Known only to inflict pain
Your appearance is attributed to a convergence of negative energy
True colors are revealed
Pass me a box of crayons and I will gladly color malicious people
How to view the world as vivid colors without negativity?
Your attitude colors the world

I Michael Collins

Self-Portrait

The sun's warmth had once seemed to blend all waters
together in one harbor; winter's star lends

only light, and ice remembers that it is
a separate temporal being, slender life struggling

to live within the patient, quiet currents
as they give it shape, their movements keeping it

translucent; otherwise he could not look down
and see the dark waves palpitate their rhythms

underneath it, could not perceive this giant,
ancient heart through that impossible eyesight

the soul guides from here into its other world,
disclosed by what imagines to contain it.

I Lydia Cortes

Wahaca Dark

There is something strange about starting at the beginning when everything's already begun nothing is new everything has been a has been seen done heard felt smelt tasted or dreamed maybe not by you but by someone somewhere sometime in this world before you even were here and there there little girl are traces of a thing or another thing or a place under the sun brother moon why don't you come out to plate a good piece of cheese or Oaxacan chocolate pronounced cho co la te the Spanish way like in Oaxaca with a capital O sounding like a W did you know that Oaxaca is a city and a state like New York New York a state of mind a state of darkness crying out for light forget the shadow boxing in Oaxaca could work in your favor if you like the flavor of chocolate not cho Ching chan change the language of the ear change your tone or your tune or your teen or your team or your twine or your twin o brother have you got a mama my mother or my sister or gots you my Papi Oh my papá my pasta my pesto my Pedro Oh my pipí peace be unto all the pipís in the world said the pope preying men... and the was the end of the story never begun at the beginning amen & hallelujah you had it coming & going to ya goodie gooey

this piece is dedicated to Puerto Rico Pa'lante Puerto Rico O mi Puerto Rico Se Levanta y Pa'lante in pieces dedicated is to Rico Pueblo siempre Rico O gente mia Lavantate Rico siempre Pa'lante Rico siempre Puerto siempre pueblo Rico de mi gente la gente mia Se Levanta y Pa'lante siempre dedicated to mi pueblo gente mia siempre Puerto siempre Rico siempre Puerto Rico Pa'lante Siempre amada

I Steve Dalachinsky

Gnostic Trio

(from the Book of Angels)

if there were angels that read books
who rode bareback
who held on tight to everything
as they sang
(to the moon to us to you)
your self a singer
if there were angels who carried
books to school each day
who waited for the school bus
just to be polite
who caressed the wind rather
than beat it
if we could all fly at least once
just for the experience & not
necessarily for the thrill
& land
books in hand
all perfect bound or
pathetically dogeared
& rest within the harp's stretched
breath
the earth(l)y desires of angels

I close my eyes
a flash of light...& I know

the poem needs you
as much as you need the poem.

I Pete Dolack

The Birds Of The Southern Plains Are Nationalists

The birds of the Southern Plains are nationalists, too
Bombarding my rental Hyundai
With a steady stream of white invective
I scrub down the windshield
But it is streaked in white again in minutes
The avian nationalists stay close to the ground
So they don't miss
Why are they so angry?
At least they are not organized
Bombing one at a time rather than in groups
Like eagles
Still they are rarely seen
Materializing for a blur
And gone
Where?
It is easy to hide in the open
I do not look for the birds
They will not be ignored in their hiding places in plain sight
My own blur an intrusion
I will wipe the canvas clean again
Graffiti artists quickly do their work again
Nature abhors a vacuum

I Gabriel Don

Swimming Lesson / Lección De Natación

"Don't pay attention to the other swimmers in the pool," they told me. Safe seeming concrete boundaries, water tamed for silly human games we called a race. But I wasn't in a pool and water was not tame and this was not a game and I was not safe. "That's when you lose," they had told me. But I had looked. I had looked into the eyes of every single competitor and realised that this was not a competition. No one needed to lose for another to win and when we lost; when we lost important things like the ground we stand on and the air we breath; when we lost the things that feed us like the people we love; when we realised the things we fought to win like money and fame destroyed the things we needed; when we lost, when we lost, we all lost.

"No prestar atención a los demás nadadores en la piscina," me dijeron. Límites concretos aparentemente seguros, agua domada para juegos bobos humanos que llamamos una carrera. Pero yo no estaba en una piscina y el agua no estaba domada y esto no era un juego y yo no estaba segura. "Es entonces cuando pierdes," me habían dicho. Pero yo había visto. Yo había visto a los ojos de cada competidor y dado cuenta de que esto no era una competición. Nadie tenía que perder para que otro ganara y cuando perdimos; cuando perdimos cosas importantes algo como el suelo en que nos paramos y el aire que respiramos; cuando perdimos las cosas que dan de comer algo como las personas que amamos; cuando nos dimos cuenta de las cosas que hemos luchado para ganar como el dinero y la fama destruyeron las cosas que necesitábamos; cuando perdimos, cuando perdimos, todos perdimos.

I Bill Evans

Tiny Orgy

Earth shattering or
Nothing, time altering
Or something
How one carries
Oneself, how one
Thinks about oneself
Yearning certainly, and
Vision, ideally/
Cut a stylish turn
Plug that in your
Anthology and take a puff
We are the stuff
Of exploded stars
Oh, that's much better –
Singular, regular, yet many

We are the stuff
Of exploded stars
I was minding my
Business at the party
Love crawling up the walls
Love ascending each
Vaporous, mental staircase
On the radio in French and a little Italian
Lone waif sailing on a plank from a land afar

Guys, are you getting this?

Out of chaos
A voice!
Rocket ship
Pirate ship
Container ship
Professorship
Ship shape
Shape shifting
Free two-day shipping
The poet's heart delivered in a box

A snack for God, and more! O citizens...

Luckily, nudity sweetens the kitty
Hark, a lark! A three-headed dog
Guarding a river --
To writhe, unbeknownst
Pitch a claim on a cot
Amongst the cuddled masses
What did I know?
Time to place one's order
And take one's chances
I'm the kind of secret that tells everybody

I Bonny Finberg

Daily News

Eve wonders what's missing,
so God pulls rank.
He's the landlord, after all,
and no one gets to occupy
against the rules.

They had a sweet deal,
Adam says.
He liked being naked,
the fridge always full,
the bottomless well of booze.
They were free from cash, humiliation –
the moral imperative someone else's problem.
She's blown it,
it's all her fault.
He complained, leading the way.

The world beyond
vast, complex, uncertain,
with limited currency,
disguises evil,
rewards the undeserving,
punishes the good,
feeds the disease.

They learn to recognize
the ground on which they stand,
to choose the proper door,
to pay the proper fee,
or perish.
But still, no guarantees.

Meanwhile, with better things to do,
God tells the fish and fowl,
cattle and things that creep and crawl,
to "be fruitful and multiply...

"...fruit of the trees, herbs of the grasses,
give forth your own kind from the seeds
contained within (your)selves."
And just for fun, he taints the apple's seeds.

"Isn't this miracle enough?" the snake complains.
"Did God make dominion?
Did Eve?
No – it was Adam.
Adam built the towers,
chose the tenants,

pays the salaries,
collects the rent.
set the terms."
For a list of all your histories,
and all the things you must avoid,
send a check for all you've got
to TimeIsRunningOut.com.
Allow six weeks for delivery.
No replacements, no returns.

❚ Jen Fitzgerald

Wildflower

I watch television shows
   where women yell

       at other women. I load
         wash and send emails

       about degeneration. My daughter
   busts through: *Mommy*

watch this bunny video. I dip
   into anxious sleep until it is time

       to make coffee. Another black
        man shot in the street. I load

       the dishwasher and send texts
   about the media

cycle-- send group texts
   about cycles.

       Once I've wiped
        clean every surface

       I retrace lines,
   stretch tendril

vines out
   over neighbors' lawns,

       cracking brick,
        dipping roots down cisterns

       in frenzied flight
   from sun light. Unknowable

space will fill with life's swell
    until I am stripped unsure

        how to draw breath,
           how to fill,

      to release,
    mend my crack to fissure.

I will call all my pieces back--
    crease their bright blue into

        a book as a pressed wildflower
           and drive to the store for milk.

I Daniela Gioseffi

Ode To Shikenah, Veiled Mother Of The Torah

I can't believe in God as love, because
He's awfully cruel at times. I wish He
were like *Shikenah*, the hidden one, Merciful Mother
who brings cookies and milk up the back stairs
to a sobbing child, after the father has
beaten or scolded the whimpering child.
Women in the story of Christ's crucifixion, weep
below The Cross, mothers and lovers of sons.
Women take the crucified body to the tomb, bathe
and shroud it, keening, praying, crying, grieving
over the son killed by other sons. The Mother is
The Holy Ghost of the Trinity, *Shikenah,* veiled one
who dare not show her face, ankle or flowing hair
least *She* tempt *Him* into life. Those who kill and hate
are angry with God the Father. They repress women,
mothers, daughters, because they bring work, toil,
warring life from their soft bellied, mammalian bodies,
veiled Mothers of Mercy, Goddesses of many faiths,
*Kwan Yin, Ceridwin, Demeter, Athena, Aphrodite
Shikenah, Liberty* marching bare-breasted, flag unfurled
leading the parade, dancing, singing ribbons
around the Maypole, while angry Puritan fathers forbid
joy, fanatical Evangelical Christians, Islamic Jihadists
repress joy, children, women, while we celebrate *Her*
cornucopia of bounty. O' Gaia, how patriarchs abuse you!
What shall we do? We wish to save your
photosynthesizing foods of *permaculture*, sans
pesticides. We bask in atmospheric balance of carbon
dioxide breathed in by rain forests, oxygen breathed out
from forest-lungs of Earth to us animals, our lives
a gift from trees. We cherish butterflies, ladybugs, bees.
We Mother Earth lovers live in gratitude for buds
from seeds opening with the cornucopia of harvests,
Fruit of the Womb to come from the *anima* of men loving,
desiring women peace makers who quell greed and fear
of the exotic other, who live by a leap of faith in life itself
without a promise of heaven, knowing Earth's pleasures,
sun, rain, sky, trees, love and joy are possible *and enough.*

❚ Barbara D. Hall

My Mother's Dream

My mother wanted to be a writer
she typed her childhood story of Sammy, the family goose
Sammy became the favorite family pet
until Thanksgiving Day
all the children refused to eat the meat
I sobbed

My mother wanted to be a college graduate
she asked her parents to help her go to college
her oldest sister warned her parents
"Don't waste your money on Nelly.
She'll just get married and have children."
I heard

Years later, after she had her children
she tried college at forty-four
she failed to make the grade
I learned not to wait

she told me
"Get your education so you
can do and be what you want
and not be dependent on others..."
I heeded

My mother wanted to travel
she talked of seeing Spain
but when she grew old and gray
the disease brought her to forget

I did not.

| Patrick Hammer, Jr.

For A Girl Not Dead Anymore

Is that you riding the treetops,
sitting on air, finally free of all
pain this windless night?
Is that you now out of the pit,
resting atop these pines, smiling?

Is that you gambolling
across the moon, that silent
oracle of light? Are you finally
alighting other worlds? Or am I
only throwing shade?

Is that you singing faintly in my ear
as the darkly handsome night
sings with its choir of crickets lit
by glow worms, among all the unseen
but sibilant creatures in the grass?

Is that you hiding and speechless now
but in my thoughts and words and dreams,
like the sleeping birds in the crooks of trees?
I know and have faith that they will be
thirsting and chattering at dawn.

I Bob Heman

The Beach

History doesn't know that you knew. They take
your words at what they say and let it go that way.
The turn of phrase, the tale that grows itself,
are taken as the words of fact that only mean
in the soggy way they act. Not the fiction of it all,
that burns through even the most mundane of walls,
making the apple that is still an apple a different apple,
and the night that covers that apple a different night,
and every bite taken a different bite, until the apple
and the night have followed the wall far out of reach,
and the beach remains still nowhere to be found.

I Aimee Herman

Dear Universe (A Manifesto)

Dear Universe, I want a full-time teaching job and at least two closets in my apartment and a complete understanding of the difference between *effect* and *affect*.

That time I asked my students to stare at each other for sixty seconds (insert laughter, discomfort and a continuous need to look away) and my student, who tried so hard to share his eyes with me, kept whispering how hard it is to look at someone who isn't speaking. And when we shared our experiences afterward, I asked him the color of my eyes; he said *silver.* Dear Universe, I want to see the shiny in me too.

Dear Universe, when did you tell me that none of this would end, that brains congeal and there is only so much a scalpel can remove?

Dear Universe, I haven't quite mastered the pronunciation of marriage and have decided to live alongside the Hadza to learn the importance of telling time through the movement of sky. Maybe I prefer monogamy with things that glow like Lyra or birds with indigestion.

I used to collect ants; scooped them up like cake crumbs and spelled out prayers with their slow-moving bodies. Dear Universe, can religion be that simple?

Dear Universe, when my ribs were the only cage I climbed into. Yes, can we go back to that?

One night when I ran out of things to hold, I gulped down enough street signs to make me feel like I understood what I was doing. Cut my tongue on their sharp edges and I still got lost. Dear Universe, my belly contains a GPS but it always brings me back to where I am afraid of going.

Dear Universe, there is a mouse living inside my oven, so I haven't cooked anything proper in months. I rolled up a poem and set it on fire hoping the ashes of words would lead it elsewhere. Like that time I read Vera Pavlova and she led me out of that mental hospital. Sometimes we just need an extra map to free ourselves from borrowed kilns or bone breaks.

I want a backyard to plant dandelions and hyaloclastite. Universe, can you give me some land to roam against?

Somehow my wrists slipped their way out of midnight and I am collecting sharps again. Like a brushfire. Like a tic-tac toe board of blood and guts. Dear Universe, I don't need any more band-aids; it's surgery time.

Remember when guns sprayed water instead of organs? I left the country of my body because my passport expired and I lost the code to get in. Dear Universe, can you leave the back door open?

I Ngoma Hill

Karma Is A B-word (Last Poem For 2016)

some things seem obvious
but hard to explain to the ignorant
too stupid to know they're stupid
that's why the president select
thinks that he can run a country
like a reality show where everything's
for sale to the highest bidder
so the pot called the kettle black
now that the hackers have been hacked
I'd say it's time for the big payback
for Libya, Egypt and Iraq
Allende in Chile, for Vietnam,
for Lumumba in the Congo and El Salvador,
for those that did not bow to Phat Sam's will
and all those leaders that have been killed
like Malcolm, Martin and the Kennedy's too
I guess you didn't pay attention to history books
or you were to young to see how fascism looks
or you just didn't care cause you're not a Jew
You didn't pay attention to wounded knee
so you don't smell the stench in the land
where nothing is free
Standing in the shadow of the grim reaper
ignoring the rule of being your brothers' keeper
and it's beginning to look like reconstruction
after the civil war
as we stand on the edge of tomorrow
staring in the face of another holocaust
with Mein Chumph at the Helm
as he tells the world to go to hell
while the inauguration had not even happened yet
and the C.I.A. could get him first
but the problem is that Pence could be much worse
So now we ask what can we do
as the rest of the world laughs at you
ashes to ashes and dust to dust

with the demise of democracy that never was
We tap the casket three times on the ground
pour libations with a little gin
may the phoenix rise from the ashes again

AsE

I Roxanne Hoffman

Rumplestiltskin

Dear sir,
but for a slip,
I might call you father
or be the son you never had,
Junior
to your Senior.
Rumpelstiltskin & Son:
Magicians and Matchmakers. Will
Transmute.
21 and
five three (on tippy toes),
I have your beady eyes. Wink, Wink.
Mother
sends her regards:
"Smiles beguile happiness,
and fictions lived daily often
come true."
You see, she too
has charms, taming despot
to princely, even cast her spell
on you —
babe in the woods,
victim of father's pride...
With all your tricks you never stood
a chance.
Lemons, sunshine —
she'll (silver haloed) own —
daily applied, spun her wheat locks
to gold.
Not quite magic?
But that's love with every
twist of her locket still upon
your neck —
she knows you wear —
her ring on your pinkie
twinkling in the sunlight, unlocks
rainbows.

I David Huberman

The Little Mouse

THE FRONT ROOM

There she appears at Charlotte's party, hesitant at first to enter, then collecting her courage at the door, she walks in with the determination of a Joan of Arc. With her gentle eyes she smiles at everyone she encounters. Absorbing every boring conversation, idle chatter, insipid gossip, listening, acknowledging the inane, the weird, the drunk, and the dull. Leaving them transformed. For once, the meek feel that they count - they hold their heads up high.

THE MAIN ROOM

The tough broads and sex goddesses look down upon her and exclaim, "Ah, look at the mild little mouse. What a harmless little creature, pity, pity to have no man of her own." Their men, slaves of lust and power, out of mere curiosity gaze at her and say to themselves, "What a peculiar little waif." Shrugging their shoulders, they turn away to smoke big expensive cigars, dismissing the little mouse from their presence.

COFFEE AND ABSINTHE SERVED IN FRANKLIN HALL

Behind the veil of sculpted alabaster shoulders, the voluptuous women sparkle with their diamonds and pearls. The men, full of worldly influence and authority, drinking their cognac and absinthe, stare once again at the mild mannered creature. They cannot escape her bittersweet image. As if by magic, a spell has been cast on them as they try to turn away, but one man unable to resist, sneaks a look. A few more follow until it's contagious. Then all the men at the party are found peeping. The one collective thought becomes, "What would it be like to kiss the little mouse on her lips goodnight?"

I Kate Irving

The Homeless And The Value Of Amber

Stranded in glaciers,
buried under sand or ash,
some are given imagined lives
by the way their bones have fallen.

Caught in a sudden plop of sap,
anopheles is interpreted with care
while other breathing,
molecular forms, aware
and visibly concealed in doorways,
defy discovery.

Exhibiting no new science or photo op,
they forage openly, bear indifference,
and speak languages of isolation.

I IsatheIntrovert

Forever

I'm the Alpha and the omega
Boss man till the end of my days used to be a lone rager. All that anger
lead to self medication and I ain't talkin' bout meditation, but rather invalidation
The loved ones that were supposed to protect me told me everything I said was
a lie
I kept my identity hidden on the inside
thoroughbred BX nigga no Armageddon where I came
I'm heavy as heaven Ain't no place like home where I learned how to hate
My mother threatened to kill her own kids to keep the dude she was wit, I refuse
to be a tragic fate
Way before I grew my beard she thought I's a waste and it's okay
She stuck in the same place
life is what you make, so I bring home to my peoples bagels and cake
When these words come out my mouth watch em' form a picture
Rembasquiapicasso rhythm staccato forever my motto n' I know I'm dat nigga
From dawn till dusk
my voice heard words bond n I'll live on even when I turn to dust
Speakin my narrative is a must in these corrupt times hope I can sweep the nation
So Generations to come will remember me behold my exaltation

I Evie Ivy

Free Words In The Air

I used to think talking to oneself was so bad.
I felt sad for those I'd hear speak with themselves
as they walked down streets and public walkways,
and halls. "Crazy" I thought. I'd look back thinking

there was something wrong there. Then after a
certain age I caught myself. After you go through
and get hit with things in life you'd rather not have
—and more than once—and can't explain it—how

they happened—you meant well—you have found
you have crossed the wrong path into something
unexpected—as time moves on, you too will walk
a street trying to figure it out, and make sense of it.

Then suddenly, you will hear your words not in your
mind but in the air, as you recap to recon with the self.

I C. D. Johnson

How NOT To Break Up With A Goddess

Dear Gaia:

There is no easy way to do this, so I'm going to just come out and say it... We are through. I'd do this face to face, but the last time we were together, your shifting moods left me with a couple of bruises.

Although I still care about you and feel that we can still be friends, I don't love you. The long of it, I've found another Goddess. Her name is Shakti. It means "Power". We're in love.

I'd like to be able to say that it's not you, it's me, but truth be told...it's you. You who are a two-dimensional imitation of the true meaning of the word "Goddess". Shakti satisfies me in ways which you never did or could. You're simply not philosophical enough for that kind of passion. Shakti also knows a lot of "Tantric" stuff. Everything there is to know about lingams and yonis (and I don't mean the musician). I'm sorry if that hurts, but you need to hear this. It's the only way you're going to understand, and I want you to understand.

Sure, we had our fun with the whole Wiccan thing and all, but there were several things that never sat right with our relationship. Your subservience to the other gods and titans, for one thing; your lack of personality, flighty nature, and plain-vanilla classical European symbolism for another. Shakti is more..."exotic". I also could never stand the way you totally sold out to the whole New Age movement.

I guess you were never really the Goddess for me. I needed a real woman to worship, not a personification. Shakti is that woman. The other gods fear and respect her. She's bold, intelligent, sexy, beautiful, wealthy, stable, more ancient than you. And you know how I like older women. Everything I ever wanted in a Goddess. Her affections aren't as unpredictable as nature. They are as constant and as concrete as samsara itself. The universe is made up of her mystery. She is layer upon layer upon layer, and I enjoy peeling them all back one at a time and getting a good look at what's underneath.

Do you know what's beneath your nature? More nature!

Shakti... I just can't stop saying her name. Shakti! Shakti! Shakti! I kind of have to share her with Shiva, but I don't mind. Her marriage to the Destroyer is simply one of convenience, and she assures me that I am her Param-Bhakta, Greatest of Devotees. Unlike you to whom I was just one little devotee among thousands. Mostly nutburgers. Your people, not mine.

Well, I'd like to spend more time and words explaining to you just how inferior you are to my new Goddess Shakti - or "Kali Ma" as she likes me to call her when we're getting intimate - but I have hymns to write and scripture to learn so I can better praise my subcontinent Devi delight, so...

Stay green, Gaia! Don't let the Climate Change get you down, and spend more time with your kids, they need your attention - and by attention, I mean abuse. See you on the flip-side!

Sincerely,

C. D. Johnson, your former devotee, the man who makes love to Goddesses, poet, philosopher, and High Priest of the Cult Of The Sacrilegious Yoni.

P.S.: Say hello to your sister Nyx for me. I always thought she was hot.

I Icegayle Johnson

Martin

Wake up Martin
Wake up Martin Luther King
Wake up DR. King

Cry over us in a loud
thunder storm spewing
people stop stop this insanity

what's the reason this continues to
rain on all the years of freedom marches
crying eyes crying crying eyes crying

remember my voice my own tears
my continous begging pleading
Martin- I heard you crying in

my dreams last night-your voice impossible
to disguise holding Heather in your arms
Heather Heyer the victium of Charlette's
violence

here's a question

Irving- I use to call god Irving
because I'm jewish- now I call him
Irving- god has no meaning or

understanding in my world- shame on you
for allowing these unnecessary protests
to fester grow become powerful rage filled

causing death's riots unnecessary violence
is this our leader promoting rage uproars
keep negative thoughts ever flowing

the universe is confused promoting
violence protesting against peace
no wonder chaos rains

I Larry Jones

Javier In Vegas

He got home Friday. He flew to Los Angeles where he saw the Walk of Stars. There is nothing else to do there. Then he rented a car to drive to Vegas. He said the Grand Canyon may have been the best part of his trip. A Nevada highway patrolman pulled him over for speeding. However he had his papers in order and was able to convince the officer that he was not an illegal Mexican alien. He is twenty-three, and as was Catherine. from Aragon, Spain. He said Vegas was all "vice," i.e., gambling and prostitution. He saw three Elvis's but not the show, "All Shook Up." I have a picture of Elvis over the toilet. Javier is rather frugal; here's another example. At a stripper club, a Cuban woman asked him what his price range was. He said all the dancers were very "high class." I laughed; he meant expensive. A three/four minute lap dance was $20.00; "Around the World" was $500.00. He said he was not going to pay for sex, had a drink and tipped the girls a very few dollars. At roulette, he lost $50.00 but they bring you all these free drinks. I asked him whether the food in Vegas was lousy, as it had been when I was there. He said that mostly they bought tacos and burritos, but once went to a grocery store where the prices were less expensive than in Brooklyn. All in all, he said he had a very nice time. I said that's nice.

I Meg Kaizu

Weeds

I sit on the windowsill
To gaze out
On the horizon
The sun dyes

My legs dangle
Over orange weeds

Insects nest
& feed
On
Nectar

I rise,
Pick up a twig,
& write
My verses
On the ground

Insects chorus
Under a spider's web
Among the weeds

I can hear
Them cast
Their spells

I Lee Klein

Expresso Bongo Florida # 7 For Dr. Phillip Solomon

To Expresso Bongo In Charriots of Freon
From high energy memorabilia
That's how I know that your there
Thought zones lit up like a neon rain forest perfectly unexploded
Before the first drop of the electrical storm falls

We ride on the murders of cooks by waiters
We ride in on the incantations -
the mango milkshakes
The poets the painters who write in our books
The swirl of the pastels, the elegance against our tattered look

If one could compose onself to got out diagonally
like an art deco cruise ship off of linear South Beach
If one could breathe fire into fire or fireworks into a troubadour

From onset to on again
Screaming driveling fearlessly
To the old whiners in leftover pantsuits
Surely ignoring this Bloody Mary haired madman
Alright as long as we have our reserve crème de menthe batteries
And the dreamscape we invoke never tiring
Of flavors of sherbet refusing on retiring
Somewhere between colorless despair
And the sunburst's fathoming of violetmarine relaxation
You rule the depths of this domain

I Linda Kleinbub

Stumbling

Thorns, thistle, be careful baby
that's her heart
soft, wet, fragile.
He looks at her
wanting to eat her up.
She looks delicious, doesn't she?

Vulnerable antique lace
disintegrates easily.
His glass shards invisible,
pierce her skin, even through
the clothes she wears.

The swallows will still fly
over the blackberry bushes
up into the maples.

She's just a girl
with tears in her belly
digging in topsoil,
planting deception,
linking memoir to history.

Jousting heart,
only she understands
this devastation.

Newly slashed her skin
pours poison, oily dark,
staining sheets
infiltrating purity.

Never play games with
ornamental lovers.

I Ron Kolm

The Emperor's Vacation

My tears disturb the dust
Of that fiery month of August —
A month as oppressive
As Caesar himself.
My suburban villa
Is in ruins
And my intestines
Portend nothing good, only ill.

I was a benevolent despot —
But the Goths have thrown me out.
Can you believe it?

The shadows of the crucified
Follow me
As I trudge down the Appian Way
Towards the Isle of Capri.
Is this then truly the end
Of an artist of such stature as I?

I Ptr Kozlowski

Force Of Gravity

It's the
Force of Gravity that's
dragging me down
won't let me fly to the sky.
Common denominator zero base root
it's all them prime numbers've got me pegged.
All those postulated principles of mathematic rage
like tiny lines tying some fat Gulliver down to the ground.
It's the
Force of Gravity that's digging all our graves
just like the Canyon of the Colorado age upon age.
I need a lighter than air craft, I need warp factor seven, I
need a law breaking genius to make new sense of the old facts
I need a death defying leap to salvation with a vengeance
I need something that I don't know what it is.
It's the
crude banality that's making me insane I wasn't
always such a screamer for a fix, but all those mass
production fashions from celebs to handi-wipes, and
all that trivial excitement they engender in the populace.
About enough to
Make you wanna
plummet to your death from some
wild place up in the Himalayas.
Force of gravity those
magic little fingers that get into every
food item on the shelf.
Force of gravity, it
calls the lonely traveler as she
reaches from the ditch for another round.
Take
history into our hands? Ha.
Take herstory into our hands? Hahaha.
Take our story into our hands? huh...
Well, actually,
Yeah.
Really.
Why not?

I Annie Rachele Lanzillotto

Pazzi Per Pignoli

the sicilian sisters dove
for the pignoli cookies
when the string red and white striped
like a barber pole snapped and the white lid
opened. "Pandora's box!" one of the men shouted.
The sisters were up out of their chairs,
groaning in ecstacy with the taste.
Normally they're composed. One's a lawyer. The other a professor.
Pignoli brings out their fangs.
I'd brought a mix of biscutt'; nocciola, pistacchio,
cioccolato, anice. Now it was war,
somehow only one pignoli at $37.50/pound
made it into the box
from the Bronx, a bite of the Bronx.
The pignoli made them pazzi.
I had moved some pignoli into the box
for my 96 year old Aunt Lucy
wanting her to taste her youth once again.
And I'd balanced one up on Mom's altar next to her lipstick.

In Sicily the Mamma of the sisters
fell again. The church recounts the three falls
of Christ right. falling, falling, falling.
We need others to pick us up. When my aunt fell
she dragged herself across the floor
walking with her elbows.
Hours, she was there on the floor.
When we can't get up on our own,
we need to be able to stay down
somewhere inside or out. We need
to be lifted, carried. The Sicilian brother stays with Mamma,
saves stray dogs, the looks in their eyes
stop me, I want to change the course
of my life for that one black dog with the white spot
on her neck that looks at me through the computer
screen. She can't see
me or can she?

The look in her eyes seems to say
You
I found.
Come here.
Sit

I Jane LeCroy

Gold Watch

Never taking a day off, never coming in late
Opa worked for Ma Bell more than 40 years-
this is how we show what we appreciate

Honored when he retired, award to celebrate
a fancy watch, number face, glass and shining gears
never taking a day off, never coming in late

Do you think a timepiece for all that Time equates?
inquires Father; the question warns of souvenirs
this is how we show what we appreciate

Opa shunned Father's music, desires and his fate
Father accused Opa of a life based on fear
never taking a day off, never coming in late

Each thought the other one was the deadweight
and swore his own politics right, absolute, clear
This is how we show what we appreciate

Father said what Mother said, to never be a slave
play hooky, daydream, create the face in the mirror-
never taking a day off, never coming in late
this is how we show what we appreciate

I Linda Lerner

So

I don't recall what Virginia town
the sight of swastikas and white
supremacists shown in Charlottesville
jetted me back to...sometime in
the late 80's...a day I heard that
that the KKK will be marching through it

a saleswoman's response who
finally appeared after I called out, "does
anyone work here?"
So, she said, when I told her what I heard
looked me in the eye for a few minutes
and said, you must be from New York"

followed me home across state lines
into a new century and a word like hot coal
I didn't feel how hot, let myself feel...

nearly a decade later, Albuquerque New Mexico:
a friend pointed to a sign in a restaurant we were in,
leave your guns here, people passed
without notice, "it's legal" someone said
who saw me staring at it, shaking my head
"in New Mexico," he repeated louder, "it's legal"

and before I could stop what couldn't be silenced
any longer, SO shot out

I Toni Mergentime Levi

Milk

Milk arrives like a blessing in my dreams –
blue-white as a glacial waterfall from a far-off thaw.
In my most joyous dream, a precious rare appearance,
I am old – old as I am now. But suddenly, my breasts
are filled with milk again and waking I remember

the neonatal ward, where my full-term bilirubin baby
looked like some blue-ribboned, beefy best-in-show.
In reality, of normal size, my jaundiced giantess
dwarfed the pink wrinkled heartbreaking preemies
riddled with tubes and sensors in their Isolettes.

They sent me home in tears, bereft, without my baby –
blindfolded in her fish tank under therapeutic light,
without *me* (impossible!) – her only known universe.
For two unrelenting days at home, my milk dripped,
useless as my love. For two years after, she drank her fill.

Milk courses through my dappled world of dream.
My breasts are swollen, tender, nipples tipped in red.
My milk is a river flowing to the land of tiny babies.
All – now *all* can emerge from their boxes, alive.
Those who said I wouldn't have enough were wrong.

I Mindy Levokove

Because

I am not the color of my hair
I am not the color of my skin
I am not the sum on my paycheck
not the bottom line in my bank account

I am not
I am not

I am not the make of my car
I am not the address on my mailbox
I am not the name on my I.D.
not the number on my social security card

I am not
I am not

I am a growing consciousness
I am a pathway for energy and light
I am a view of endless choices
I am a conduit in a universe of change

I am
I am

I Eleonore Ley

Sonnet #1

Don't let them say your opinion is shit
Read up, speak up, make them listen to you
Your brain and everything in it is it
Nevertheless she persisted, fuck you
The world is the reason I'm so angry
Old men telling me I'm being bratty
The world is the reason I feel beauty
Earth, Skies, Trees, Women's Solidarity
If you ever feel like love is loosing
Look into the eyes of an animal
Love or hate is a matter of choosing
Kindness the best way to feel beautiful
The brilliant thing is, kindness and anger
To change the world, do wonders together.

I Tsaurah Litzky

Birthday Poem - August 31 2017

I can't find my favorite bra, the only one that fits me well,
the black padded one I got at the Goodwill for $2.99,
the one that makes my bosom swell like I am thirty-five,
although my breasts are heading south to Miami.
I want to wear it today as I enter my seventy-fourth year
because desire still blossoms in me like suds in beer,
desire like an everblooming jubilee
sets me free like Venus rising from the sea.
I'm so grateful.
I've looked for it everywhere, in all the drawers,
the bathroom, the bedroom, in the dirty laundry.
Oh, there it is! Over there! Under my writing chair!

❚ Ellen Aug Lytle

Still Dressed For Heat

'I perceive that ghastly glimmer is noonday sunbeams'
from aids memorial (poets) park

a circle lights the sky tonight; hope
from a great cloud and wan sun dwindle
a pinpoint second leaves me begging for a beach,
as if it's home, and that Thursday,

during a September rain in the village,
where all the love I ever felt washed me while I walked,
even wet socks falling into my shoes didn't matter, reaching
him is what counted

same as those lost autumn evenings, when
leaves pasted on street trees
hadn't yet fallen
till now

when seeing grizzly sundays polished
and the snow across a bald field and humped hill gloat,
like an iced intruder, i'm the one dressed in beads, though
costume bracelets make up

the lack of a love that turns humming into song

yes, we are leftover women, our child far behind, pushed out
of the way, after someone steals the perfect pudding;
a love fantasy roiled yet asleep in the round
somewhere between heart and a mind

still dressed for heat

I Stan Marcus

The Short Guy

The short guy in my knowledge
is enamored of the tall guy,
and so they lie down together,
a Mutt and Jeff, and I
wonder how such an awkward
arrangement has happened.
These old friends over
the years who have mated
how many times still
wait for the opportunity to do
so again. I can picture the act
but lack sympathy, and why
should I have any? It's not up to me
to define. I'm incongruous in my own delights,
supple and slippery, and I suppose
there are those who cannot imagine
what I do. I strive nowadays to be
inexplicable, to satisfy my yearnings,
if not at the spur of the moment
at least potentially. So long
have I given myself nothing,
reargued my position over and over
until I was thoroughly convinced
that deprivation was a kind
of outline. I could live wholesomely
inside it, never despairing
because I had accepted what
was not mine. Suddenly I see
license, or gradually saw it,
and now I have questions that
install me squarely among others.
A kind of drowning in freedom
from which I needed protection,
so I constructed a small garden
I could traverse in an hour.
What can I do now? I seem to have

discovered desires and lost
myself. How can things be so open?
To act is simple—to restrain is impossible.
My poor garden is as beautiful
as ever but has become a fiction.
I lust after circumstance,
to be eternally baffled,
to say for the moment,
"No, I have no idea what I mean,
but I've spoken and I refuse to retract it."

I Jesús Papoleto Meléndez

The Flood Came To Puerto Rico

The flood came to Puerto Rico/
unexpected/   unwelcome
like american tourists
& it left   like american tourists:
taking all & leaving nothing.

the flood came to Puerto Rico/
& with it came geologists
　　/they are trying to find new names
　　for the many lakes & rivers
　　that now exist
　　where towns once were
　　where homes once stood
　　where people once lived
　　where children once played
　　in the warmth of afternoon suns
　　where the beautiful culture
　　that is mine once sang   sang
　　its loveliness over the hills & mountains.

the flood came to Puerto Rico/
& american airlines are taking pictures
for their advertisements of their new lagoons
where the kennedy family will vacation
this summer/   next summer
all year round.

the flood came to Puerto Rico/
killing my people
drowning them in a new form
of oppression/
leaving them jobless/   homeless
to the mercy of american kindness
with begging hands in the air
with tears in their eyes
with crying & dying babies

65

in their arms/
    leaving them with less
    than what they were known
    to ever have

    lost/
    separated from
    their mutual loves.

the flood came to Puerto Rico/
& with it came the red cross
    /after the flood
to search for *Donald Trump's* golf courses
             & summer homes.

I Nancy Mercado

Epilogue For The 21st Century

And the demon took possession of the nation
Leading it by the hand in circles
Engaging in topsy-turvy talk
Weaving and unstitching gnarls of lies
Dangling morsels of doubletalk and innuendos
And the nation jumped
In attempts to capture those morsels
If only for a second
To distill them into reality
To identify them as black or white
But the demon
kept changing the meaning of all things
Kept morphing his empty shell
Of broken bits of shinny chards
Of wickedness enshrined in glassy vials
And the nation contorting and heaving
Drowned in a melee of arguments
And weapons
And hurricanes
And earthquakes
And wildfires
And special reports
On the evening news
While the demon's henchmen
Went out into the world
And defiled the rivers
Defiled the women
Defiled the poor
Defiled all the good creatures of the earth
They were hell-bent
Maniacal in their derangement

They were the leaders of the free world.

| Alejandra Moreno

May Flower Of The Cloud Forrest

Sweetness of Columbia,
Flor de Mayo, bashful, bittersweet La Mojana.

She trips over the glades,
The peculiar, fickle mythical being!

The buds unfurl their perfumed mugs
For we adore her sweet ego;

And silver-feathered creatures start to tune their throats,
While wind-chimes loan their rings to La Mojana's enchanted choirs.

Fetching Mayo, shy, meditative Lady,
Sitting among a court of lilies
And apple blossoms that perfume the breeze.

Orchids, Orchids, Orchids, Orchids,
Rich, fragrant, ephemeral!

Dance in the rainbow rain shower!

Was there ever so candied a blossom?

"I'm the breath of life, May they call me.
Sunset's redden hue is not as memorable
As the blessing of my sprout so uncommon.
I am God's benefaction to the forlorn."

I Dennis Moritz

Walking The Williamsburgh Bridge

if you make it to the next stop near here
if you keep your voice and announce your health
if you feel keen one on one
if you make it feel it want it how much
*

palms of hands soles of feet peeling shoes
over the bridge walk thud no place to sit
the curve up the curve down now a center
when there's rain or snow
*

eddie wishnack froze learning to drive right there
on the egg crate grill roadway of this bridge/twisting
the steering grabbing tires/eddie wishnack a boxer
bobbed and weaved the punch that gets you puts
you down always a left hook dimly glimpsed
*

when the senses close down it's death we're done
but we spoke to my mother said we love/all is remembered
what is forgiven/everything/when you thought
I thought/when you moved away and I moved
forward/when you traveled back in memory
I was stuck/still/in the present
*

everything significant ends up peripheral
a wham hit from somewhere else not figured
not yet felt until all perceptions arrive unannounced
whamming along the side of the face/do we
then turn with or away snap back at it/

I KB Nemcosky

Early Exits (Excerpt Pages 107-108)

Helpline rant from Exec. V.P.
in middle of a crisis gone viral

"What's so funny! Are you
laughing at me? You're laughing
at me!

I can have your job for this!
I've seen you in the hallways!"

> We carry Neanderthal DNA
> found in our lip prints on water
> bottles leeching estrogen-like BPA

Big hair guy at Bongwater concert
says he's "mad, bad & dangerous
to know" – Lady Caroline said
that of Lord Byron in 1812

> Such is depression – one overcast
> afternoon, I decide to bring birds
> to alleyway – hang 2 birdfeeders
> on fire escape – to my surprise
> their elegant plumage is
> overwhelming

Neighbors complain how their
terraces are being pelted by shit
from my god damned birds –
outside my door a bucket
scrub brushes & another note

▌Yuko Otomo

More Description Of Our Kitchen Wall (For Myself)

I hate the circus
I do not like zoos either
I ignore time, most of the time
I love an (open) field
I detest gossip
I love my name,
especially the way it's written
in my mother tongue

I thank my parents, the earth
for bearing with me

I am cosmos

I am not into angels
but I care for them
when they are broken
as I love a sad-faced woman
when she is quiet

I understand a man's need for friendship
I think it is beautiful when 2 men walk
together in light

I love to rest by a clear brook
when I am tired
I give all my emotions to the sky
I respect clouds
in any form with any speed

I am not good at games
likewise, I am still confused
over how to use keys
I respect thinkers
when they are accurate, kind & pure

I enjoy the lingering sound of a bell most of all music

I cherish the found objects of this city
we carried home together
I am glad we agree that
Rembrandt did not need to paint a peasant woman
behind the magnificent carcass

I am fascinated by my own fate
of the agony & ecstasy of living
with this red brick kitchen wall

especially when the wall becomes a mirror
& a mirror the world

▌Eve Packer

We'll Get Used To It

we'll get used
to
it
we won't even
notice
we'll get used
to the dictator, caudillo, strongman
boss by edict, executive action, fiat,
we'll get used to it, we won't notice
'alternative facts', lack of checks
and balances, erasure of three branch
government, zip freedom of press, no open
door for immigrants, no roe vs. wade, no healthcare
insurance
we won't notice
the girl kids dying bloody
coathangers up their pussy, the kids
w/no parents, the parents w/sick
kids, spike in asthma, smog,
pollution, the sleepers on subway grates,
sleepers on the subway, the breakdown
in the subway, the round-ups and shootings,
radioactive holocaust, the hurricanes and
sharp winds unending, the dead polar bears,
the dead seas and hummingbirds, the planet
on fire--

it won't be us, it won't be our daughter
fever and bloody sepsis, it won't be me
sleeping on the subway grate, it won't be
my hijab caught & ripped at the gate, it won't be
my son, grandkids rounded up, it won't
be us
caught in nuclear bombing, drowned
city we'll get used to it we won't even notice:

we're dead

▌D.Bird el Palabrero

Toes

"Excuse me,   sir?
   Hi,   sorry
I just want to bring
      to   your   attention
You stepped
          on my toes.
Could you please   watch
      Where you're going?"
"I stepped on your what?"
"Toes,   sir.
You   stepped on them."
"Well I don't see   toes, I see   people."
"Clearly,
that's part of the problem.
You didn't see where you were going
And,   perhaps   inadvertently,
Stepped on my toes,"
"I didn't   step on your toes
You're just part of the   radical   leftist
      pro-toe agenda
that's making you   snowflakes   so
overly sensitive"
"Yes,   to gravity
Also,   your foot,"
"Look buddy,   I couldn't have possibly stepped on your toes
      My wife,
          has toes,"
"Why are we talking about your wife's toes?!
I thought you said you didn't even see toes
      GASP
You have a toe fetish,
it all makes sense now..."
"Look asshole,
I don't see   my wife   as somebody who has toes
I look past   her toes"
"So,   does she have to make them invisible?

75

Do   you make her wear socks in bed?
What about the socks that have   toes   in them?"
"Hey,   I'm not a bad guy!
I'm   a   sensitive
Nature   loving
Warm,   compassionate
Donated my Sunday mornings to feed   the homeless
Obama   and   Hillary voting
    Guy!
I'm   not   the problem!
Your   toes   are the problem!
  Fuck.
      your.
        toes!"

And that's what it's like to talk to white people about racism.

I Puma Perl

Bodega Alley

It's 9:45 PM November 17th; I'm almost home after walking the two miles back from the poetry workshop. In the Bodega Alley the men wear shorts and sit on beach chairs. I saunter by in my gloves and hat and leopard scarf and we don't say hello and we don't not say hello. There is a tacit agreement - don't fuck with me and I won't fuck with you. I wish that all of my relationships were as manageable.

I realize as I cross Madison Street that I've not seen another woman since Grand, other than the one rushing off right now. She's with a raspy-voiced guy; he's telling his friends be right back, wait, don't go nowhere. Clearly they are up to something on the menu of no good. I've not seen another woman, but I've also not run into any rats, making it a good night; any night is a good night if you avoid the rats. It's become a rarity, a night without rats. Last week, I fought off a pack of them by furiously swinging my coat and umbrella. The rats are one reason why I do not walk these streets clad in shorts and flip-flops, and would never sit half dressed on a folding chair in the Bodega Alley.

It's 9:52 PM; I enter my building softly, careful not to awaken security guard; he's sleeping peacefully, head on yesterday's Daily News, hand wrapped around his cell phone. The elevator is waiting. It's 9:54 PM when I put my key in the bottom lock. It's 9:55 PM, the computer informs me, when I step inside.

And this is how time goes, one minute meaningless without the others lining up behind, or leading the march.

There are no clocks in the Bodega Alley.

Everything remains the same.

I Howard Pflanzer

Harmony Hotel

Harmony Hotel
Pleasant living
Space for the world.

Always a bed
Always a girl
Always a guy
Whatever you want
You got it there.

Hot water
Or cold
Peace or
Pandemonium.

You got it there
No questions asked
No requests refused
At the Harmony Hotel.

I Su Polo

Spell

The spell of the bass
Everybody's playing
But the bass is weaving the spell.
Vibrating tones
Blending with your soul
Puts a spell on you.
I've fallen under that
Spell before;
The mystery of sounds
That fold you in,
Up and down
And then,
There you go.

❙ Ron Price

Above Nothing Below No One

for Daria Colette

The cold broke
Today, ice, snow
Melting –

Oh, I know, none of it's meant to honor the warm breath
Your voice brought to my ear.

You sleep now in my arms
Having grown almost too big to hold.

Daria, my heart, I would hold you
Until a final flash ends everything we know and love.

I measure our days by your laughter,
Each giggle another blossom
In a flowering that will forever be
Crocuses in snow.

May your home be scented with sandalwood
Blessing each loneliness for the taste it takes you
Into the shared breath of all creatures,
Even dogs.

I wish for you more than flowers,

Struggles that make you
Stronger each time they break you.
Love you feel no matter how distant the source.

May your tears bless you beyond blossoms
Into fruit.

▌Zero Prophet

AmeRican

i am
a panhandling man
tin or aluminum
they call me tha king a can
i'm known
stoned on my garbage thrown
home is a battle zone
not no pure-white-clean poem
i reign
crowned on a downtown train
pain is my main domain
lock stock and rusted chain
i rule
this NuyoRican school
stole me the jewelers tool
the sun still shines for the cool
my grind
recycled re-defined
degraded graffiti sign
void unemployment line
my vow
to live in tha viet now
almost asimilao
misshapen scrape and bow...
my health
mis-diagnosed myself
Stolen stealth on a shelf
caught in tha common wealth
refuse(d)
recycled residues
barrio babaloos
hand to mouth hard time blues
I deal
straight outta potters field
all that I feel I steal
gotta keep it surreal

my vice
dreaming with loaded dice
bullet proof beans and rice
drunk or just junkie christ
my skill
chasing that dollar bill
racing up san Juan hill
willing to Kill, Kill, Kill
my high
aguanile mai mai
Ashe on tha loisai
accent on the ay ay ay
so free
spic in the master key
Po' Rican obituary
Jose can you see, see, see
I'll die
Fly in the friendly sky
spittin' in the storm's eye
Lai le lo lai le lo lai....

I Leslie Prosterman

Intervals

There is music in the spacing of the spheres: Pythagoras

Hold on to the back of my
iridescent blue Schwinn.
Steady me, I am six.
You are twelve.

We banked our bikes
around the same curve,
over and over,
following the sun
in perfect
silent synchrony.

Records spun Belafonte indoors
and Cyril Richard reading
from the new salmon-pink boxed set:
Alice in Wonderland.

We paraded
as we listened:
plod, sink, rise, turn,
eyes glazed,
passing each other unseeing
on the cushions of a small tweed sofa.

I am more than fifty-six and for over twenty years
now he strides blindly among the asteroids.
His corneas give sight to the eyes of someone
who needed them more than

he

and I pedal unsteadily,

alone with him,
my bike edging ahead of his black Raleigh,

now one, now the other

passing, unseeing,

he humming faster and higher pitched
always a bit larger now in the farther distance

we

freewheeling

singing our own fractured harmony

❚ Jill Rapaport

Julie Christie Rides Again

"Blood in sheds" turned out to be "blond in shorts", and the grassout was grass and dirt. Lavender was strong. One can see in what profusion the wrong ideas germinate.

Still the farmhouse was open and a blue blade of grass ruled it, and the orange, "jolly purple," and brotherly gold of the southlands surrounded it blazing.

[Mention the drab downplaying of really good ideas (as a countercompensation), and the infernal myth of its beauty (unawares).]

Sandrew barreled ungracefully down the steps carved into her hilltop castle and threw herself onto Sylvie, the donkey they rode to town.

The Chorler Indians and Lesser Pelicans of Montup Island busied themselves with resting in the temporarily delicious sun, especially because you won't have time, nor P. VII, the ridiculous colonial governor shaped like a tamale and a spare cloth being waved from the tower. The blue with a little green was not jolly. The B. car, or the A. car, depending on how solely you want to recoup your investment, sits you out back near an unexpectedly pretty and nostalgic stream in which, at one blow, romance, bananas, that blond in shorts and the lavender grass and dirt, tea, jam, "Shan't we live together ever again?", secret animals, Carthage and Thrace, rich parks, Chicago and Thrace combine and recombine tumbling over the rocks in conquest, blue, a little green, some orange, the inferior breeds and the major ones, a farmhouse lifted and tilted on the shoulders of a red ant, moths, "tapettes," but not too close to one, unless of course one is one, a beautiful woman who turns out to be you, shyness and aggression all together over the washed pebbles, the sly lizards underneath the surface, in the morning sun, the evening moon, as in a thunderclap of creation, except that it is more like the lullaby of evolution mixed with dialectic and a healthy rage [expostulate some and some more . . .], and pears, apples, golden apples and golden harmonies, the apt distribution of all the needs of the living, and no more of the living than need live, all sit on the thread of one rollicking ride down the stream, and looking up, you see that contrary to popular opinion, V. can occasionally get somewhere on time, because she's here, with bare eyes and head, tanned feet, the short pants that they are wearing this season and a hobo's crushed hat that when she sees you eyeing it she takes off and gives you.

I Carlos Manuel Rivera

Goleta En Nueva York

A: Federico "Fico" García Lorca, mi Pana.

Vengo
de aquelarres,
donde los arrecifes
y macarras
baten aguaceros
desde sus tortillas,

y por donde el canto
con bisagra
cunde
ánimos
en alfarerías.

Aproximo
a naipes
sin sus antesalas

que con taconeos
de centellas
curvan
ronroneos,

donde la arena
del misterio
contonea sus sainetes.

Cuadro
por allende
los mares

un solo
silencio de kif
que polvoriza
la Alhambra,

atolondra
sequías
desde rascacielos,

asoma
desde mi goleta
interludios,

a pocos pasos
de entre
ínsula/península,

y revuelca
de Eros
fronteras

a un Tánatos
que sus pamplinas.
comienza.

I Renato Rosaldo

Looking For Lorca

I.

In Granada, Federico Garcia Lorca,
name of airport, the cultural center, park,
a museum, once his family's summer home.
Inside: a wooden desk, his theater company's poster,
his drawings, photographs, his piano.
Fitting tribute, the city's favorite son.
But remember August, 1936,
his murder in nearby hills next to an olive tree,
Franco's Falange determined
to make Spain great again.

II.

Twice they look for him at home,
find he's with friends, lock him up,
then one obscure night fascist assault guards pound
on the jailhouse door, *en la puerta golpeaban*,
pirate the poet in an automobile,
force a confession:
socialist, Freemason, homosexual.
Headlights glare,
Lorca still in pyjamas,
military orders, instant firing squad
formed by locals—civilians and police,
When challenged, the Generalísimo declares,
"These are natural accidents of war."

III.

Seven years before the fact, Lorca writes
prophetic verses, "I realized I'd been murdered,
but they never found me."
Atrocity breeds opacity.
Archeologists, forensic anthropologists, historians,

eye witnesses, journalists, bulldozers search
for remains, come up with only maddening murk.
Local legend, pride laced with shame, stitched
for eighty years, whispers
what nobody knows, says, one night,
a month after his execution, Lorca's family lifts
body from shallow grave, buries
it under their parlor, humming his deep song.

I Robert Roth

Untitled

A former Playboy model surreptitiously filmed an older (to me younger) woman in the gym and made some smarmy comment about her appearance. She posted it on Snapshot writing, "If I can't un-see this then you can't either."

She insisted that it was a spontaneous act of malice she just had to share with a few friends. Not something she expected to go viral. But it did.

Relentless fury, outrage and contempt came down on her--"Body shaming" "Fat shaming"--until she couldn't leave her home. The words of criticism were very accurate. But the relentlessness of it, the magnitude of it, the underlying rage and cruelty was the same. Only the target had shifted.

Things will never change if vindictive glee is the only power people allow themselves to feel.

I Thaddeus Rutkowski

From Nowhere To Nowhere

Every morning, the radio on top of the refrigerator in my family's house played the top hits. My mother was the one who turned the radio on. She liked music, and sometimes she would sing back a song.

Out of all the hits, the one that stuck in my mind was "Nowhere Man." The melody hooked me, but the lyrics didn't mean much. I certainly lived in a Nowhere Land, but was I a real Nowhere Man? Was I a man at all, or just a boy? I definitely felt like a boy. Did I have any Nowhere plans? I certainly wanted to leave Nowhere and get Somewhere. Would I be able to do that, or would I go from Nowhere to Nowhere?

I knew where Somewhere was. It was in the shows I saw on television. Where I lived was not on television, and the people I saw on television didn't come to where I lived. That would have helped, if some TV actor showed up where I lived. That would have proven I was Someone. But I knew no TV actors. I was No One.

I didn't have high expectations; I just wanted to get to school on time. The radio had a clockface that told when it was time to leave.

One morning, I heard my mother singing "Nowhere Man." She had most of the words right. When she stopped singing, she said, "It starts out well, then it repeats. But it doesn't go crazy, like most of the songs I hear."

My mother left for work just before my siblings and I left for school. She walked out to meet a driver in a car pool. Shortly afterward, my siblings and I slammed out the door and ran for the school bus.

I K. Saito

Twin Nose Dirt

Foolish Short Animation;
This is for people in modern, busy society.
Which is bombarded by various concepts.
The momentary vacuum out of the ordinary,
whose meaningfulness turns meaningless.

Title; Twin Nose Dirt
I'm interested in a silly art.
Why?
Because I have discovered my own self who was excited and amused the most.
What on earth is this?
Perhaps, it reflects an adult's unexpected silliness.

I Sarah Serrano

My Communion Is Not Your Oppression

praise falls from my lips
as I look to the sky
I think how can I not worship these wonders

why should I be restricted
worship a god created by men
when my womb and spirit answers mother nature's call

do not build your church on words from past lovers
your stained glass windows will crack
steeple will crumble
parapets turn to dust

build your church with words your soul whispers
to your spirit
while you sleep

this will be your communion

I Ravi Shankar

The Acorn And The Hungry King

> He, in sleep, in imagination, dreams of feasts, closes his mouth on vacancy, grinds tooth on tooth, exercises his gluttony on insubstantial food, and, instead of a banquet, fruitlessly eats the empty air.
>
> - Ovid's *Metamorphoses*, Bk VIII:777-842 (translated by A.S. Kline)

The voice inside the oak sings a high tannic note,
bitter and herbaceous like squashing a sodden

teabag on your tongue until your throat contracts
in revulsion. Those who say its song rounds out

a good sherry, ignore repressed memories of blood
inside the wood, the trauma of the swung axe blade

in Ceres' coppery grove where the Dryads once held
their ancient sacred dances, writhing under votive

tablets and garland wreaths. Bite into an acorn,
and you can taste the faint sweat of those nymphs,

before the aftertaste curdles your stomach with fire.
Desire, the Buddhists advise, *ta hā*, that Pali word,

remains unquenchable, bottomless, a belly ravaged
by famine, like the curse that befell old Erysichthon,

the Thessalian king, when he felled the massive oak,
then fell himself, first ear-sick, then heart-sick,

then forever ravenous, munching the air to breathe,
swallowing whole olives, pit and all, sucking honey

from the bees' hives and milk from the very udders
of his royal cows. The more he devoured, the more

he had to devour, but it was like pitching drachmas
into the Aegean, if the coins were wholly immaterial

and the ocean infinite. He drained each amphora,
only to grow thirstier. He ate until he had his fill,

and he never had his fill. Finally, he began to gnaw
on himself, beginning with his digits, then his hands,

then his very arms up to the elbow and beyond,
crunching bones and sinew. Isn't that the meaning

of craving? The nature of addiction? The hunger
sunk deep inside of you that tries and tries and tries

and tries, but can't get no satisfaction? The dead man,
as a living man, devours a dead man, himself, still

alive, but slowly, surely, dying in excruciating agony.
That's us burning coal and hacking down rainforests.

That's us at the turn of the millennium. Think of him
next time you order a particularly oaky chardonnay.

I Yuyutsu Sharma

There's A Treasure

There's a treasure
in my warm bed

a velvet touch
of swallows, a scent
of rhododendrons,
two moons and a Sun,
a song of mellowing kisses
I've fantasized
in half a century
of my short life

wild canyons
an abode of snow
a sanctuary
of a million shrines
and jubilant gompas

and down below
a delta of rainforests
where icy waters
of life and longevity flow.

I Susan Sherman

The Tears Of Things

Will they cry for us when we have gone
the objects that adorn our lives
When we have left   will they miss our touch
our need for them

Do they know they are the chosen ones
or do they fear we will tire of them
set them aside   bound as they are by our desire
not theirs

A ball point pen   white   with gold bands
imported from France   birthday gift
from a beloved friend   A fountain pen
sun yellow with black enamel tip
Relics of an earlier age

Forty Oz books hidden from prying eyes
Well worn novels   books of religion
philosophy   the occult   long out of print
All those books we hold dear   have kept through years
with leather bindings   colorful illustrations
childhood dreams

Even the magazines we treasure   worthless
to others   A college t-shirt   now sizes too small
A pair of boots   useless   but prized
A turquoise necklace from an old lover
too full of memories to wear

All the things we refuse to throw away
Each one holding a piece of our past

No longer here   people may cry for us
but even those who hold us dear
at a certain point move on   Our objects
belong to us alone   We have left part of ourselves
behind in them

Lacrimae rerum: the tears of things
Do they love us as we love them
Will they weep for us when we are gone

I John L. Silver

On This Dark Afternoon

on this dark afternoon
I saw into the rain
your illuminated image
reflected in wet cobbles

as the water grew deeper it sustained
a temporary equilibrium
above the grate

I thought of you leading me
into your journey of no direction
to your door of surrender

our complexity of circumstance
was so convincing

you said you wanted
to pay your final debt
to get rid of it all

your final reach for freedom

perhaps in a singular location
where the beginning of all
ends accumulate

I Joanna Sit

Timescape: Wonderland

(To Susan Montez, one year after her death)

The choice had always been: love
or love, word or whip. You saw yourself

in the wooded pond, reached out
and touched your own terror, beauty
distorted even before you fell

Who was there? On the other side
of the water was madness

where the hatter grimly sat
with the hare, bowl abrimmed
with meat pies, scones

to nibble on while you passed
through the gate, slid yourself
behind the picnic table --

Your tongue tied like Dante,
you wanted to drift with Allen
in a field of poppies.

Instead, you were cast down
into a story without a wizard
to help you home

Still, you were not sorry,
just thirsty for the salt,
and a little tearful at

the promise of amnesia,
saying goodbye to wine,
whiskey from heaven was not

easy when all was lost
and you recede, reappear,
one movie into another,

into that glassy indifferent world
that made you invisible, final,
your body broken like rain,

given over to the stars, left
to eat your own words, to wander
from one desert to another, looking
for a place to lay your head.

I Angela Sloan

Butcher's Peppermint

Sally is precise in folding the fresh meat in white paper
Making sure not to stain the package with traces of blood and fat
A patron's child – a young boy with eager hands –
Causes the blue jar of fat peppermint sticks
Adorning the countertop
To topple and crack open
The patron slaps his son's cheek and jerks the package away
"I can't take you anywhere!"
The boy, embarrassed and weeping, his face red from being struck.
Sally shouts for Ira to bring a broom
She collects each peppermint stick, blows away the grit and hair
Sweeps up the glass, careful not to embed an invisible fiber into her hand.
That night, while Ira is asleep, she steps into the bathroom
Examining the triangular blue shard
She slides a strap of her white eyelet nightgown down over her shoulder
And holds the blue memento to her left breast
Sinking its sharpest point into her flesh
Blood wells at the wound; she wipes the redness away.
She wraps the glass in a handkerchief
Turns out the light and returns to the bed she shares with her husband.
She eases into sleep
Listening to the rhythm of his breathing.

❙ Miriam Stanley

John Robert Lewis

He was pinned to God.
The way a mother pins a child's address onto a coat.
Or an exile carries a suitcase for his elderly father.
There is not much else to do but grasp the obligation.
So when he came to Pettus Bridge,
blocked by policemen with raised batons,
He flew forward into the bloody sticks.
Cast like Jonah into the whale,
for he had a message to send to Nineveh.
Nothing was going to keep him back.

I Laurie Stone

Smoke

My sister's hair has grown back. A young man passes in Birkenstocks, a shaved head, and dreadlock payes. The tassels of his tallis flap below his white sweater. I sit with my sister on the porch of an empty house. The door is the pale gray of a sick tooth. Jeanne Moreau died today. Her mouth turned down as if she would always be sexy. I see her stepping into a French taxi, the window cracked so she can smoke. When drugs destroy tumor cells, you are a "survivor." When drugs do not destroy tumor cells, there is no term. A man on the street is collecting plastic bottles, wearing one pink glove. My sister is taking prednisone for her cough. People fall in love with her hands. She can chop a brick in half. At summer camp a girl started speaking to me in Yiddish as we rode along on horseback, a slim, thirteen-year-old girl with shiny blond hair. The horse boys wore their hair in duck tails and rode with a swagger, their chests thrown out. They whispered to the horses with flirty clicks. When my friend started speaking Yiddish, I kept saying, "What?" even though I understood what she was saying. Everyone has ideas about what to do in Iceland. They have the same ideas: White sand, white foam, white snow, white dogs. I remember departures more than arrivals. The future of two relationships is behind me. When I think about my sister dying, I remember fireflies we trapped in a jar and kept alive with wire mesh for air and grass for food. They flickered until we set them free. Recently I had coffee with a man I had been married to. We had not seen each other in forty-three years. He recalled an affair he had had with one of my friends, a beauty with high cheekbones and full lips. I had slept with her boyfriend. I said to the man I had been married to, "You said she bored you." He shook his head and said, "I told you that. I didn't want to hurt your feelings." At the base of a tree on Columbus Avenue are a banana peel, a styrofoam egg carton, and a soiled bra. The roots of the tree rise up like thick fingers forming a fist. During the time I was married, I rode a lambretta scooter and wore aviator glasses, and long skirts that brushed dusty ground. As *Game of Thrones* heads toward a finale, my interest wanes. No one cares how anything turns out. When our brother was thirty, he came to stay at my sister's house. He wanted to leave the woman he was married to, and he was thinking of drowning himself in a small, nearby lake. My sister said, "You'll have a job of it. It's all silted up, and you'll have to wade out a long way to get any real depth." Our brother's head moved back, and he laughed. The more unfinished, the more freedom. On the TV show *Jessica Jones*, the title character does not eat. She drinks instead of being sad. I want to see her eat. I want to see her pouty lower lip encircle an apple and suck up noodles. My sister says, "I am eating chicken with Russian dressing before my tastebuds go." She looks glamorous with an amused expression on her face. I feel like a dog running away and coming back. I'm not far from your doorstep.

❙ Zelene Pineda Suchilt

Waiting For Sun

Just the moon and I, again
down 5th Avenue past my old house in East Harlem

I heard Hector Lavoe making love to Ruben Vlades

but they didn't have sex!

They just walked to the park and talked about being singers,
Vlades even wrote a song about it and Lavoe stole it!

I kept El Periodico de Ayer because it's a reminder that it happened

they really wrote ese pegron!

Pero qué más se puede hacer?

But to walk down Fifth Avenue and watch squirrels cross the street with cars coming,
Because they believe in public love,
In birds and things, one finds inside Frida's house.

Everyone loves Frida but they forget she lived in constant state of pain.
They say her garden was beautiful, Transplantes from Oaxaca, La Matriarca
And I believe them.

I surrender to the rain speaking to the concrete with steam and a scent
The secret yeast of a rising sun
Majestically misunderstood

It's hard to explain that type of weather,
When they're both out at the same time
Dancing silently quietly, but for the rain that whispers:

Sun, I want you, I could no longer wait to see you and I'm sorry.

I am my mother's daughter and my father's hundred years of solitude
His father's town relied on incest to keep the race
But five kilometers down grandma's hips made voodoo.

When you chop peppers & onions
There is a near certainty
that the chemistry that
makes them special will
float upwards and
catch your
eye

I Terese Svoboda

The Dukes Are Up

At the gated manger,
we three kings empty

our arms, still hopeful
in our outstretched-ness.

So the gifts flopped,
with a cancel on future orders--

there's still win-win on every face
when we leave. We shuffle off,

our traditional bathrobes
falling open by the time

we reach the first oasis
and somebody says,

laughing, the dukes are next.
And there they are,

hirsute, pink-faced,
not a wobble among them.

What ho, they shout. *The stars
confused the heck out of us.*

We point with our sandwiches,
we share coordinates, *Take your time*

we say. The haboob is already
lifting the sand to blot out the way.

❚ Alice B. Talkless

Trumpet

My business controls the decade now,
although inconsistent with any known value
and unlike anything you've ever seen
under the hashtag "democracy",
which I consider deportable.
Your vote was never something I'd need.

Nor will I make it my duty to hear
or acknowledge you in any way.
Health and education are meaningless -
'only a job' matters to a slave.
I do not pledge to withdraw high fences
or motion sensors, or a well-armed gate.

My power was forged with the money
it took to buy one judge or one republican's
fate. Agenda; to close forever
a constitution built for naive colonials.
I will implement a national post-truth tweet -
a sweeping revision of your all-time low
into an elite American great.

I J M Theisen de Gonzalez

Untitled

Tucked into an already off-beat resume was my gig as a school photographer's assistant chiefly at Catholic girls high schools. Things hadn't changed much since my tenure at such an institution--girls still roll up their skirts at the waistband; have intensely whispered conversations about boys, sneak courtyard cigarettes, and don't see the endgame good of doing Spanish homework. Watching the students' unguarded moments, I'd mused about their futures. There was a wholesome sweetness to their concerns. These girls were funny, smart young women far savvier than their parents fathomed. Some girls would have intimidated the hell out of me at school. But watching them sit for photos; seeing their desire to please, to be all their parents expected, what their teachers reckoned, while remaining cool enough for their friends was rather poignant. Observing their coltish energy while preparing themselves, I overheard things that dumbfounded me. The big surprise was that they didn't see how they were such beautiful creatures and school photos represented a fraction of what they offered to the world. Many said, "I don't like to smile; I don't look good when I smile." Where did they get that idea? A few said, "My mother said she's got enough pictures of me--we don't need more." Ouch! That plugs directly into low self-esteem and comments like that are the ideal diet to feed that feeling. One girl really concerned me. She declared that her boyfriend wanted all of the photos. I said it was nice that she had someone who cared so much for her. A classmate came in, and she told the previous night's tale, which involved a pre-paid cab ride to and from Staten Island to hang out with a smitten guy not her boyfriend. I'd thought about that girl, hoped she sensed her value, and realized that seeking affirmation in someone else's eyes is a shortcut to feeling better about yourself in the long run. As well as the concept of fidelity in relationships. I also wonder if any of those girls ever look back on those photos and what is reflected to them. Are they still flawed and unpolished? Or do they at last see the finished work from the sketches of the accomplished young women I found before me during those afternoons.

I Tim Tomlinson

Careful

Lately I find myself unable to sleep.
I look up at the dark ceiling. I stare at the dark ceiling,
at the shadows that move across the dark ceiling
when a car's headlights sweep past
Frank Crosetti's driveway—

the driveway with the child's bicycle
with the training wheels and the bell on the handlebars
and the faux-straw basket fastened to the handlebars,
the basket ornamented with figures from Disney cartoons.
Cynthia's bicycle. Darling Cynthia.

They put blocks on the bicycle's pedals so her short legs could reach.
She liked to stand as she pedaled, her downstrokes
originating all the way up in the ribcage,
not from the hip and thigh
the way they do in experienced cyclists.

She was always coming back from some place
with objects in her basket—sticks, cans, sometimes wildflowers.
Once or twice she gave me something from the basket.
Whatever those things were,
I don't have them anymore,

but for very short moments
they gave me pleasure.
I stare at the dark ceiling and try to recall those objects,
how I slept on those occasions when Cynthia gave me objects
from the basket, months, even just weeks ago.

Nothing.
I doze off in a half-sleep. I have half-dreams,
half-dreams that startle me awake.
In one, my wife discovers what I have done,
but I know she never will.

I have been that careful.

114

I Edwin Torres

No Yoyo

(he's from New York) ... (from Puerto Rico New York) ...

(he's a New Rican) ... (what they call a Riqueño) ...

(bein' New) ... (or Trigueño) ... (Speakin' New or Rican) ...

(a Nuyo seekin' No Yorker) ... (is he new) ... (or a Porter) ...

(a port?) ... (of sherry) ... (Cheri Cheri) ... (Porto Puerto) ...

(York, oh) ... (Yoko?) ... (Coco!)... (que hablas) ...

(se habla Coco?) ... (no'co) ... (no city) ... (port of

no city Rican) ... (a Porto Ric'er is called) ... (a bori'cuer) ...

(a Boricua) ... (a boring'wha?) ... (a bore) ... (this is boring) ...

(into my yawner) ... (what 'chu saying) ... (what New saying) ...

(the New Say) ... (be the New City) ... (of York) ...

(a yorkie) ... (a pit) ... (a bull) ... (a toro) ... (a Torres) ...

(a city nono) ... (a city Yorker uncorked) ... (a boozer?) ...

(a bozo) ... (a New bozo) ... (yo soy bozo) ... (in the YO zone

si) ... (yo soy the NEW Yo) ... (that's some NEW Yo, bro) ...

(yo Rican, si) ... (soy No Rican) ... (he's No Rican) ...

(from No Ricua) ... (he's no You) ... (no Yo) ... (no I) ...

(the I) ... (in I) ... (is the NEW No) ... (I be) ... (some o'dat) ...

(NEW No) ... (from No Ricua, bro)

I Ewan Turner

Pomegranate #7

The day they first met he had spilled pomegranate seltzer on his pants so all afternoon in the blazing heat, his legs were sticky and swampy.

Sitting together at the crest of the mountain as friends explored their own internal/external wastes, she confessed that she too enjoyed pomegranate seltzer and that all things considered there were worse things to spill on a garment of clothing.

They held hands as the sun went down behind the holy hills which he had visited in youth, but at the time had seemed so boring and colorless, on long car rides with Dad before Dad was too old for road trips and rarely left the house.

Back in their city they congregated kindly, the importance of friends—their initial mode of contact, falling away. It was only them, a happy couple of lovers now sharing an apartment where space was an issue and a cat, her cat slept in his bed but didn't much like him.

The cat, a tawny orange creature with ghastly green eyes always took her side when they fought, climbing onto her lap in the midst of a domestic skirmish to purr and nuzzle in her arms. Infuriating. So too were the unwashed dishes on her day, his leaving of the toilet seat open, peeing with the door ajar, constituting her pet peeves.

Bottles of pomegranate seltzer they had bought to drink in celebration became flat in the unwashed and dirty fridge.

One morning he awoke to find her gone. The cat and its litter were gone too. A note was on the fridge that said "Till Next Time," and he smiled even through the sadness which was fast approaching. He drank the flat bottle of pomegranate seltzer and contemplated other lives.

I Claire Van Winkle

Double Process
for Courtney

In our world, red meant a day-old bruise, or the stain
of some capricious siren's lips, or blood
with all its potential taint. But every six weeks,
when Courtney would take the night off to dye
her hair its famous gilded scarlet, crimson became
the myrtle crown of our Orphic rituals.
When her double-process was complete
I would anoint our lips with wine and drown
my hands in the breaking waves of her hair,
its ecstatic swells dammed by all my rough palms
had to offer: gentle teasing and the entheogen
of an all-natural conditioner. I would finish
our maenadic day by taming her wild curls, binding her
tresses in an ascetic French twist, and freezing the upsweep
with Elnett Satin—
a spray that could hold firm all night long
but would disappear, as advertised,
at the *single* stroke
of a brush.

I George Wallace

I Open My Eyes

like a wound which opens up its mouth and lets love in, I open up and close my eyes;

like the dying wings of a gypsy moth, dusty, dying, like the eyes of a sea bass cast up on the dock, lungs caved in, sideways on the dock and dying in the salt gray, dull and dying and slow;

like a woman in the bedroom dark, visioning her long lost perfect lover, I open my eyes and open and open them, I let darkness flow through me like riverwater;

like shouts and curses of stevedores grappling along canals, like rope and hooks and rats, and broken whiskey bottles on the quay, like river otters at play, splashing, spitting back at the wind;

like the steamships carrying cocoa and oil to north america, and factory workers flowing through factory doors;

like no more dredging, no more spillage or fear;

I open my eyes and close them, like the pages of a holy book, like sugar cane burning, like a falconer at the gate, the wounds of the heart, the plow and the soil;

o sweet harvest of blood, I open my eyes, loins joined with the loins of the earth

I Phyllis Wat

Dog Picture

Dogs Are Not Allowed
I verify
first that I am
not a dog
walk in, buy the paper

behind a fence, on the grass
DOGS ARE NOT ALLOWED
I am not a dog
there either

signs make fun of dogs
because dogs can't read
slowly I realize
owners can
with leashes

the picture
dogs cannot
exercise free will
follow their noses
where their noses take them

I feel sorry for dogs

I Bruce Weber

Between The Wars

you remind me
of the years between the wars
when love surrendered easily
and time fluttered its wings
like a bat out of hell
it was then that you came to me
carrying on
about the weight of his refusals
about the glimmer in his eye
about the terrain of his tempestuousness
leaning on the table
with a heavy fist
and dreams broken
like eggs
on the hotplate of the sidewalk
staring into some blank abyss
where the clocks hands
turn unmercifully
in endless circles
and women curtsy
and men pin carnations on their lapel
and the sun sets in the morning
and nighttime is alive with colored shadows
that recline in the tubes of the painters
and geneva purrs on with business
and a glass raised to neutrality
and the skeleton bones
of the helpless dead
slip under the white sheets
of the morgue
and the windows open
and the bodies jump
and the streets are scarred
with the war dead
and you stretch your hand out
shaking off kindness like a leaf

slinging apologies like soft bullets
reminding us of time's follies
and the wicked playthings
with their jagged elbows
love breaking mirrors
love climbing to the roof
love storming the barricades
love sleeping in the park
love joining the folds
of life together
like busy ants
running
into
the
pyre
of
the
day

I Francine Witte

Charley Explains Baseball To Me

and how it's about history,
game six and Gehrig and so many

stats. I tell Charley that history
hasn't been kind to him and me,

and I remind him about the night
he hooked up with the ice cream girl,

and how I forgave him because booze
was already the other woman. Of course,

I say this only in my head. Charley stopped
listening long ago. And I think about leaving again,

and again, I think how easy life could be, how
just like the clean smack of the bat or a baseball

birding through the sky. And that's when Charley
tells me how he could've gone pro. Star catcher

in the pee-wee league, and later scouted
in high school, but the damn drink hooked him

early, easy fish. He takes a deep breath
and says he'll tell me more later, and

I settle back in for the evening, looking
at the boy that lives in Charley's face.

Jeffrey Cyphers Wright

Artwork: "Let's Play", drawing and collage, 2017

APPENDIX

A:

Austin Alexis: poems, fiction and nonfiction in **Clockwise Cat, Brownstone Poets Anthology, Brevitas Festival, Nassau County Poet Laureate Society Review, The Ledge, Home Planet News, Poets 4 Paris, Lips, Chiron Review, The Lyric, Rabbit Ears: TV Poems, The New Verse News, The Unbearables**. One-act plays at **Theater for the New City** and **Boog Festival**. Book: **Privacy Issues**. austinalexis3@ twitter.

_____

Joel Allegretti is the author of, most recently, **Platypus (NYQ Books**, 2017), a collection of poems, prose, and performance texts, and **Our Dolphin (Thrice Publishing**, 2016), a novella. In addition, he is the editor of **Rabbit Ears: TV Poems (NYQ Books**, 2015), the first anthology of poetry about the mass medium.

_____

Merissa Anderson a native New Yorker of Italian and Puerto Rican decent. She is a sociologist and currently working as an assistant project manager for the **Bogotá Audiovisual Market (BAM)** in Bogotá, Columbia which holds its film screenings event every July. She also worked on this year's **ANYDSWPE** anthology as an assistant editor. **http://www.bogotamarket.com/**

_____

Madeline Artenberg's poetry has appeared in many print and online publications, such as **Vernacular** and **Rattle**. She won **Lyric Recovery** and **Poetry Forum** prizes and was semi-finalist in the 2005 contest of **Margie, The American Journal of Poetry**. Her work often touches on Jewish and New York City themes. **The Old In-and-Out,** a play based on her poetry and that of Karen Hildebrand, directed by Kat Georges, garnered raves in June, 2013.

_____

B:

Yael Baron is a Performance Artist and a Mental Health Advocate and Activist. She has appeared on stage and in other venues including: **Brooklyn Wildlife Summer Festival** at the **Living Gallery, Verses Against The Drug War** at **Gamba, Show Me How to Smile/Rise Up To Stigma** (at the **Opera Center of America**).

_____

Steve Bloom is a life-long social activist who lives in Brooklyn NY and works as a decorative painter and faux finisher. His work has been published on numerous websites and in various journals and anthologies. Steve has no academic degrees and has won no prizes or awards. You can find out more at **www. stevebloompoetry.net**.

_____

Peter Bushyeager's poetry collections include **Citadel Luncheonette** and **In the Green Oval**. Recent poems in **Live Mag!**; the **Unbearables' From Somewhere to Nowhere**, and the forthcoming issue of **Local Knowledge**. Reviews and articles in **Rain Taxi, Encyclopedia of American Poetry/Twentieth Century**, and **What is Poetry (Just Kidding, I Know You Know), Wave Book's** anthology of **Poetry Project** interviews.

_____

C:

Patricia Carragon's latest books are **"The Cupcake Chronicles"** (**Poets Wear Prada**, 2017) and **"Innocence"** (**Finishing Line** Press, 2017). She hosts the Brooklyn-based **Brownstone Poets** and is the editor-in-chief of its annual anthology. She is one of the executive editors for **Home Planet News Online**.

_____

María Fernanda Lara Chamorro is a black Ecuadorian poet having performed her work at **New York City's 2017 Poetry Festival, MoMa PS1's New York Art Book Fair, John Jay College**, and more. She is a recipient of **CantoMundo, Callaloo**, and **VONA** fellowships. Her poems and translations have appeared in **Kweli Journal, The Wide Shore**, and elsewhere. She lives in Washington Heights.

_____

Tina Chan is a lively poet whose writing style is a poetic enigma. She believes words ejected from the heart can make a difference with consequences.

_____

Michael Collins poems have received **Pushcart Prize** nominations and appeared in more than 70 journals and magazines. He is also the author of the chapbooks **How to Sing when People Cut off your Head** and **Leave it Floating in the Water** and **Harbor Mandala** and the full-length collections **Psalmandala** and **Appearances**.

_____

D:

Poet/collagist Steve Dalachinsky was born in Brooklyn after the last big war. His poem **"Particle Fever"** was nominated for a 2015 **Pushcart Prize**. His most recent books include **Fool's Gold** (2014 feral press), **a superintendent's eyes** (revised and expanded 2013/14 - **unbearable/autonomedia**) and **flying home**, a collaboration with German visual artist Sig Bang Schmidt (**Paris Lit Up Press** 2015) and **The Invisible Ray** (**Overpass Press** 2016) with artwork by Shalom Neuman.

_____

Pete Dolack is an activist, photographer, poet and writer who wishes he could keep all those balls in the air but, alas, keeps dropping some of them. He writes the **Systemic Disorder** blog and is the author of **It's Not Over: Learning From the Socialist Experiment**, an analysis of the 20th century's socialist experiments written with an eye toward doing it better in the 21st century.

_____

Gabriel Don raised in Australia, Singapore and Dubai, a wanderer currently living in Loisaida, published in numerous online and print venues, expresses herself in a variety of ways: Art. Collage. Paint. Drawing. Performance Art. Music. Writing. Poetry. Film. Editor. Interviews. Events. Photography and teaches writing at **Pace** and **BMCC**. – **https://www.facebook.com/gabrieldoninnoparticularorder/**

_____

E:

Bill Evans lives in New York City. His book of poems, **Modern Adventures**, is published by **Spuyten Duyvil** and is available on Amazon.

_____

F:

Bonny Finberg's fiction, poetry and photographs, published internationally in literary journals, anthologies, and gallery exhibitions, include a story collection, **How the Discovery of Sugar Produced the Romantic Era** (**Sisyphus Press**, 2006); a novel, **"Kali's Day"** (**Autonomedia** 2014) **Déjà Vu**, poetry and digital collages (**Corrupt Press** 2011); **Sitting Book** (**Xanadu Press** 2017). She received a 2014 **Acker Award** for fiction.

_____

Jen Fitzgerald is a poet, essayist, photographer, and a native New Yorker who received her MFA in Poetry at **Lesley University**. She teaches creative writing online and around New York City. Her collection, **The Art of Work** was published by **Noemi Press** in September of 2016. Her work has appeared in such outlets as **PBS Newshour**, **Boston Review**, **Tin House**, **Salon**, **PEN Anthology**, and **Colorado Review** among others.

_____

G:

Daniela Gioseffi is an **American Book Award** winning author of 17 books of poetry and prose. She has won 2 grant awards from **NYSCA**, **The John Ciardi Lifetime Achievement Award** in Poetry, and reads widely. Her latest book is **Waging Beauty as the Polar Bear Dreams of Ice** 2017. She edits **www.Eco-Poetry.org** that receives 6 thousand global visitors monthly.

_____

H:

Barbara D. Hall, author of **"Waiting for the Bus: a poetry chapbook"**, **Adam's Eve**, **Sadies Secret** and the **Stuffy the Cat Series**. **www.ournaturematters.net**.

_____

Patrick Hammer, Jr.'s recent book of childhood memory poems, **BRONX LOCAL**, is available on Amazon. His next collection, **PARAMUS LOCAL**, will also be available shortly.

_____

Bob Heman's words have appeared recently in **New American Writing, Caliban online, Otoliths,** and **The Other Side of Violet [great weather for MEDIA]**. "**THE BEACH**" was first published in **No Roses Review.**

_____

Aimee Herman is a queer performance artist, writer and teacher with two full-length books of poetry, most recently **"meant to wake up feeling"** (**great weather for MEDIA**). Aimee is also a singer and ukelele player in the poetryband **Hydrogen Junkbox**. Aimee's poem **"Dear Universe (A Manifesto)"** was first published by **great weather for MEDIA**.

_____

Ngoma Hill is a performance poet, multi-instrumentalist, singer/songwriter, Artivist and paradigm shifter, who uses culture as a tool to raise socio-political and spiritual consciousness through work that encourages critical thought.

Ngoma weaves poetry and song that raises contradictions and searches for a solution to a just and peaceful world.

Ngoma is the **Beat Poet Laureate** of New York for 2017-18.

_____

Roxanne Hoffman worked on Wall Street, now answers a patient hotline. Her words can be found in cyberspace, set to music, immortalized on the silver screen, and bound in print. She runs the small literary press **Poets Wear Prada** with Jack Cooper. Her elegiac poem **In Loving Memory**, illustrated by Edward Odwitt, was released as a chapbook in 2011.

_____

David Huberman is the Ranter and the Raver of the Lower East Side for the past 30 years.

_____

I:

Kate Irving's chapbook, **"Raising the Arsonist's Daughter from the Dead"** was published by **Finishing Line Press**. Her poems have appeared in **BigCityLit.com, qaartsiluni, Press 1, Over the Walls, What Comes Next,** and **Tamarind Magazine**. She's a native New Yorker.

———

Bryan Cornel Fox (IsatheIntrovert) is a New York poet who loves to box and has performed poetry around the city at places such as **Nuyorican Poets' Café, GLBT Center, Word at 4F,** and the **Bowery Poetry Club**.

———

Evie Ivy, poet/dancer has 3 books out, **The First Woman Who Danced**, poems based on her experiences as a dancer, **Living in 12-Tone . . . and other poetic forms, No, No Nonets . . . the Book of Nonets,** (which has become her personal favorite). She has work in webzines, **Levure littéraire, Versewrights**, etc. Evie hosts the long running **Green Pavilion Poetry Event** in Brooklyn.

———

J:

C. D. (Seedy) Johnson: The editor-in-chief and publisher of the **ANYDSWPE** annual anthology series through **Rogue Scholars Press**, New York. Former web developer, webmaster, and I.T. Director for **CEO Clubs International, Inc.** Currently, a freelance web, software, graphic design, and digital publishing consultant. Tutors disabled persons in the use of computers and hands-free technology. Holds an M.A. in analytic philosophy and logic theory and a B.S. in computer science from Old Dominion University. Has taught adult literacy classes, introduction to philosophy and logic, Advaita Vedanta philosophy, and religious instruction in Sanatana Dharma and Shaktism at the **Shiv-Shakti Peeth** in Hollis, Queens. Current projects include books on philosophy, research into Indian Nyaya logic, and "constructed language" theory. Seedy is also the founder of the **Philosophy Φ** discussion group on Facebook.

———

Icegayle Johnson, multi media artist. **"the key"**, 2012. Anthology, **"TV poems"**, 2015. Forth coming,**"Room # 1408"**, 2017"

———

Larry Jones was the co-producer along with Bruce Weber of the first five **ANYDSWPE** events at **Café Nico**, his loft apartment / performance venue one flight above the **Pyramid Club** on Avenue A. An Associate of the **Academy of American Poets**, his work has appeared in many literary magazines and anthologies. He teaches literature and creative writing to gifted and talented youth at **Hofstra University**.

_____

K:

Lee Klein (born November 30, 1965) is a poet, curator, essayist and writer on the arts.

_____

Linda Kleinbub is a poet, journalist, and painter. She is a native New Yorker, a lifelong resident of Queens. She is a co-founder of **Pen Pal Poets**. She is a mentor and committee member of **Girls Write Now**, an organization that works with at-risk high school girls who are interested in writing. Her work has appeared in **The New York Observer, The Brooklyn Rail, Yahoo! Beauty, Front Porch Commons, Grabbing the Apple: An Anthology of New York Woman Poets, First Literary Review-East**, and **The Best American Poetry Blog**.

_____

Ron Kolm is a co-editor of **From Somewhere to Nowhere: The End of the American Dream** and a contributing editor of **Sensitive Skin**. He is the author of **Duke & Jill, Night Shift** and **A Change in the Weather**. He's had work in **Maintenant, Local Knowledge** and the **Outlaw Bible of American Poetry**. Ron's papers are archived at NYU.

_____

Ptr Kozlowski has been a taxi driver, deliveryman, poet and printer, singer-songwriter and guitarist. Published in **Hobo Jungle, Stained Sheets**, and **South Florida Poetry Journal**, anthologies from **Great Weather for Media** and **Performance Poets Association**. Performed at **CBGB, Bowery Poetry Club, ABCNoRio, Cornelia Street Café, Brownstone Poets, Saturn Series, Silver-Tongued Devils** and the **Conklin Barn** in Huntington.

_____

L:

Annie Rachele Lanzillotto's **"Hard Candy: Caregiving, Mourning and Stagelight"** and **"Pitch Roll Yaw"** are a two in one flip book, from **Guernica Press** 2018. Lanzillotto's **"L is for Lion: an italian bronx butch freedom memoir"** (**SUNY Press**), was a **LAMBDA Lit** Finalist. Her first collection of poetry **"Schistsong"** came out from **Bordighera Press**. Lanzillotto's is a singer/songwriter. Listen to her albums and audio books. Links at: **www.annielanzillotto.com**.

_____

Jane LeCroy is the front woman in 2 very different bands on **Imaginator Records**: **The Icebergs** (vox, cello, drums) with the album **"Eldorado"** and, Ωⵎ**(OHMSLICE)** (vox, modular-synth, drums, horns) with the album **"Conduit"**. Get them from **Bandcamp** / listen on **iTunes, Spotify, Apple, Amazon**, etc. Follow her on **FB/ IG-**, join her list at **www.janelecroy.com**.

_____

Linda Lerner – **A Dance Around the Cauldron**, a prose work consists of nine characters during the Salem witch trials brought into our own times (**Lummox Press**, September, 2017) nominated for a **Pushcart Prize**. Previously **Yes, the Ducks Were Real**, (**NYQ Books** (Feb. 2015). Her next poetry collection, **Taking the F Train,** will be published by **NYQ books** in late 2018 or early 2019.

_____

Toni Mergentime Levi is a poet and prize-winning librettist. Her poetry collections include **White Food** and **Watching Mother Disappear** (both **Mayapple Press**) and **For A Dancing Bear** (**Three Mile Harbor**). Her poems have appeared in anthologies and dozens of journals; she has been a resident fellow at the **MacDowell Colony** and numerous other artist colonies in the US and abroad.

_____

Mindy Levokove is a multi-media performance poet: a member of **Brevitas**; she sings for peace and dances for water. Also, she teaches qigong and Tai Chi at **Northern Sky Kung Fu School** and Adult Literacy and Math at the **Lehman College ALC**.

_____

Tsaurah Litzky is a **Pushcart Prize** nominated poet who also writes fiction, erotica, memoir, plays and commentary. Her poetry collections are **"Baby On The Water"** (**Long Shot Press**) and **"Cleaning the Duck"** (**Bowery Books**). She is completing a new poetry collection **"We Shake it."** Her memoir, **"Flasher"** will be published this winter by **Unbearable Books/Autonomedia**.

_____

Ellen Lytle has 2 chapbooks, 1 book of poetry, 1 book of short fiction– still teaches writing on Staten Island, still loves and weeps over every injured animal, still has hope for humanity, and maybe a book of her newest poetry from **NYQ Press** will come out soon; Maybe!

_____

M:

Stan Marcus lives in Montclair, New Jersey.

_____

Jesús Papoleto Meléndez, one of the founding members of the Nuyorican poetry movement, is the author of four volumes of poetry, most recently **"Hey Yo/Yo Soy - 40 Years of Nuyorican Street Poetry**, (2012). He is also a playwright, whose play, **"The Junkies Stole The Clock"** (1974) was the first Latino play produced by **Joseph Papp's New York Shakespeare Festival – the Public Theatre**. He has been awarded a **NYFA** grant (2001) and a **NEA-Combo** grant (1988) in poetry.

_____

Nancy Mercado is the recipient of the **American Book Award for Lifetime Achievement** from the **Before Columbus Foundation**. Editor of the **Nuyorican Women Writers Anthology** published in **City University of New York's Voices e/Magazine**, she is also a guest curator for the **Museum of American Poetics**, and assistant editor of **Eco-poetry.org**. For more information, go to: **nancy-mercado.com**.

_____

Alejandra Moreno is a history major and performing artist from Bogotá, Columbia. Along with Merissa Anderson, she worked on this year's **ANYDSWPE** anthology as an assistant editor. She's expecting her first child in the spring.

_____

Dennis Moritz has written 30 plays. Venues include the **Public, Nuyorican, Bowery Poetry Club, Poetry Project, LaMama, Freedom Theatre, Painted Bride, Theatre Double, Theatre Ariel**. His second collection of plays will be published by **United Artist Press** in Spring 2018. His play, **Just the Boys** was anthologized in **Action: the Nuyorican Poets Café Theatre Festival**. Thank you Miguel and Lois.

_____

N:

KB Nemcosky has authored three books of poetry: **Drift (Ten Pell Books**, 2000) and **dear friend, (Straw Gate Books**, 2012) and **Early Exits (United Artists Books**, 2018). His poems have appeared in **Tamarind, The Unbearables Collection, Pagan Place, Gathering of the Tribes, Press 1, Push New York**, among others.

_____

O:

Yuko Otomo. Japanese origin. A bilingual (Japanese & English) poet & a visual artist. She also writes haiku, art criticism & essays. She has read in **St. Mark's Poetry Project, Tribes, Bowery Poetry Club, ABC No Rio, La Mama, The Living Theatre, PS1, MoMA, The Queens Museum**, etc & in Japan, France & Germany. Her publication includes **"Garden: Selected Haiku" (Beehive Press), "A Sunday Afternoon on the Isle of Museum" (Propaganda Press), "PINK" (Sisyphus Press), "Small Poems" (Ugly Duckling Presse), "The Hand of The Poet" (UDP), "STUDY & Other Poems on Art" (UDP)** & **"Elements" (the Feral Press)**. She exhibited her artwork at **Court House Gallery @ Anthology Film Archives, Tribes Gallery** & **Vision Festival**, etc. She is a contributing writer for a collective art critical forum **www.Arteidolia.com** currently. Yuko is a 2017 **Pushcart Prize** nominee.

_____

P:
Eve Packer: bronx-born poet/performer/actress. 3 books from **Fly By Night Press**, 5 poetry/jazz cd's, teaches at **WCC**, mom, grandmom, lives downtwon, swims daily. (evebpacker@aol.com).

_____

D.Bird el Palabrero is part poet, part comic, and all anti-hero. A graduate of the **School Of Poetic Arts** and the **Full Circle Ensemble**, his work has been described as a kind of Puerto Rican Experimental Theatric Poetry. D.Bird has been featured at poetry events throughout New York City, including **Inspired Word**, **Capicu Culture**, **Oye! Avant-Garde Night**, and the **Nuyorican Poets Café**.

———————

Puma Perl is a performer, producer, and a widely published poet/writer. She's the author of two chapbooks, **Belinda and Her Friends** and **Ruby True**, and two full-length collections, **knuckle tattoos** and **Retrograde**. She is the creator and curator of **Puma Perl's Pandemonium**, which merges poetry with rock and roll; as **Puma Perl and Friends**, performs with some of NYC's best musicians. Puma is a recipient of a 2016 **Acker Award** in the category of writing, and of two **New York Press Association Awards** (2015 and 2016) in recognition of her journalism.

———————

Howard Pflanzer is a poet and playwright. **Dead Birds or Avian Blues (Fly By Night Press**, 2011). Publications: **And Then, Downtown Brooklyn, Tribes, LES Festival of the Arts, An Unnatural Election, Word: An Anthology by A Gathering of the Tribes**. Hybrid performance piece, **Walt Whitman Opera**, adapted from Whitman's poetry, music by Constance Cooper, presented at **undergroundzero festival**, New York.

———————

Native New Yorker Su Polo is an artist, poet, singer, songwriter, player of guitar and dulcimer and computer graphic artist. She is curator and host of the **Saturn Series Poetry Reading** and **Open Mike** for 24 years every Monday night in NYC. **Turning Stones** and **Beauty** are her Chapbooks. Her website is **Supolo.com**

———————

Ron Price is a Teaching Artist at the **Juilliard School**. He is the author of **Surviving Brothers, A Crucible for the Left Hand, A Small Song Called Ash from the Fire**, and **A True Account of the Failure of Bodies to Adequately Burn**.

———————

Zero Prophet aka Not4Prophet is a Po' Rican poet, seditious singer, militant MC, anti-corporate agitator, and an indignant Independentista. He has released several indie music albums with his bands, **RICANSTRUCTION** and **X-Vandals**, and is currently the singer/emcee and songwriter for the all mighty **ABRAZOS Orchestra**.

———————

Leslie Prosterman, author of **Snapshots** and **Dances (Garden District Press)** from which Intervals comes, and poems in various journals and collections, collaborated with composer Charley Gerard to set her poem **FluteBone Song** to music, now out on CD (**Songs of Love and Passion**). A former academic, now a community teacher of poetry, she is also a sometime student of trapeze.

———————

R:

Jill Rapaport's collection of fiction, **Duchamp et Moi and Other Stories**, was published by **Fly by Night Press / A Gathering of the Tribes** in 2014.

———————

Carlos Manuel Rivera -– Poet-performer, actor, Professor at **BCC, CUNY**. He won the First Prize in the **International Contest** of the **Puerto Rican Institute of Culture**, 2013 in the Essay category with the book **Para que no se nos olvide. Ensayos de interpretaci n sobre un teatro puertorrique o marginal (So we don t forget: Essays of interpretation of Puerto Rican marginal theater)**.

———————

Renato Rosaldo has published three books of poetry, **Rezo a la mujer aranya/ Prayer to Spider Woman** (winner of the **American Book Award**), **Diego Luna's Insider Tips**, and **The Day of Shelly's Death**.

———————

Thaddeus Rutkowski is the author of **Guess and Check, Violent Outbursts, Haywire, Tetched**, and **Roughhouse. Haywire** won the **Members Choice** Award, given by the **Asian American Writers Workshop**. He teaches at **Sarah Lawrence College, Medgar Evers College** and the **Writer's Voice** of the **West Side YMCA**. He received a fiction writing fellowship from the **New York Foundation for the Arts**.

———————

S:

K. Saito
1948 Born in Okayama-City, Japan
1990 Moved to New York

_____

Sarah Serrano is a Puerto Rican Artist, Educator, and Hakuist from Bushwick, Brooklyn. She currently writes with **The Haiku Guys**. She's written for Drew Barrymore, performed for **Latina Magazine, Prudential, Madewell**, and featured at the **Nuyorican, The National Black Theater**, and more. Catch Sarah traveling the world with her red typewriter while writing personalized poems. Keep in touch with her @CantFightTheFro.

_____

Pushcart Prize winning poet Ravi Shankar is the author/editor of over a dozen books, including most recently **"The Autobiography of a Goddess,"** translations of the 8th century Tamil poet/saint Andal and winner of the **Muse India Translation Prize** and **The Golden Shovel: New Poems Honoring Gwendolyn Brooks**. He currently holds a research fellowship from the University of Sydney.

_____

Yuyutsu RD Sharma, recipient of fellowships and grants from **The Rockefeller Foundation, Ireland Literature Exchange, Trubar Foundation, Slovenia, The Institute for the Translation of Hebrew Literature** and **The Foundation for the Production and Translation of Dutch Literature**, Yuyutsu RD Sharma is an internationally acclaimed South Asian poet and translator.

More: **www.yuyutsu.de, www.niralapublications.com**

_____

Susan Sherman: Most recent books are **Nirvana on Ninth Street**, short Fiction with photos by Colleen McKay and **An Afterward by Rona L. Holub (Wings Press,** Fall, 2014); **The Light that Puts an End to Dreams: New and Selected Poems (Wings Press**, 2012); **America's Child: A Woman's Journey through the Radical Sixties**, a memoir (**Curbstone / Northwestern University Press**, 2007). She has survived living and writing in the East Village / Lower East Side for over fifty years.

_____

John L. Silver – Grew up Cold Spring Hbr. Long Island. Read Rexroth and other beats early. First published in High school literary magazine **New Dimensions,** Wrote in college (Penn State). Hung out with poet Steve Horel & became interested in the poems of John Haag. Also became interested in Blake and W.S. Merwin. Eventually ended up in the Village. Painted in Tompkins Square Park. . Also did many covers for **Tamarind**. Started writing more. Became Host of **Tamarind Collation** for about 10 years. Moved to Westbeth. Published in **AND THEN, The National Poetry Magazine of the Lower East Side, Handsy** on line, **Long Island Sounds,** and in other anthological formations. Published 2 books of Poems, **Empty Pieces, (Underfield Press)** (2016) and **Poems From a Trembling Road** (2006) (**Underfield Press**) also Contributed and did covers for **White Rabbit.**

Joanna Sit is the author of three books of poetry: **My Last Century** (2012), **In Thailand with the Apostles** (2014), and **Track Works** (2017). She is currently working on an ethnographic narrative about Chinese immigrants and Cantonese opera.

Angela Sloan received her MA in English and Creative Writing in 2012 from **Longwood University**. She now lives and writes in New York City. Her previous works have been published by **Three Rooms Press**, most notably in their 2016 anthology celebrating Millennial fiction: **Songs of My Selfie**. Angela is also a regular contributor to **A Gathering of the Tribes.**

Miriam Stanley has a new collection of poems published by **Rogue Scholars Press**. Its title is **Driving The Celexa**. She has three previous collections of poems published. Ms. Stanley also has work published in numerous anthologies.

Rebelené (Zelene Pineda Suchilt) is a CHí-CHí (CHilanga/CHicana) award-winning storyteller and political organizer living in New York City.

Terese Svoboda has published 17 books of poetry, fiction, translation, memoir, and biography. Last year **Professor Harriman's Steam Air-Ship** appeared, the year before **When The Next Big War Blows Down The Valley: Selected and New Poems**. "Terese Svoboda is one of few contemporary American writers who possesses a global consciousness." - **Brooklyn Rail**.

_____

T:

Alice B. Talkless is Ronna Lebo, a poet, musician and painter who has performed in the NY scene for over twenty years. She is co-founder of **Black Square Editions**, a non-profit press for poetry and art. She is also co-founder of **Reservoir Art Space** in Ridgewood, Queens, which includes private studios and an experimental gallery for visual arts.

_____

Edwin Torres is the author of 7 books including **"Ameriscopia"**, **"Yes Thing No Thing"** and **"In The Function Of External Circumstances."** Edwin was the first recipient of **The Nuyorican Poets Cafe Fresh Prize For Poetry** in 1991. His next collection, **"Xoeteox: The Infinite Word Object"** will be released by **Wave Books** in 2018.

_____

My name is Ewan Turner and I am a BFA student at the **New School for Drama** with a focus on creative writing. Recently, I published a chapbook of poems called **Sotapanna** and have read my work, both fiction and poetry at venues including **KGB Bar**, and **Berl's Poetry Shop**.

_____

W:

Claire Van Winkle is a poet, essayist, and literary translator. She currently teaches creative writing, composition, literature, and grammar at **Queens College, Borough of Manhattan Community College**, and the **Fashion Institute of Technology**. In addition to her creative and academic pursuits, Claire works as a Recreational Therapist (RT) at the **New York State Psychiatric Institute**. Her clinical work and research focus on the development and implementation of Pedagogical Therapy, which applies linguistic theory and creative writing workshop methods to one-on-one and group therapy sessions for inpatient psychiatric patients.

———————

George Wallace is editor of **Poetrybay**, co-editor of **Great Weather for Media**, and author of 31 chapbooks of poetry. He is writer in residence at the **Walt Whitman Birthplace**.

———————

Poet Phyllis Wat is author of **Shadow Blue, The Fish Soup Bowl Expedition, The Influence of Paintings Hung in Bedrooms** and **Wu Going There**. Wat is publisher of **Straw Gate Books** and an editor, **The World, 6ix magazine** (receiving 2 PCA grants) and **Press 1**, online. She is recipient of a poetry grant from **Pennsylvania Council on the Arts** (PCA).

———————

Bruce Weber is the long time organizer of the **Alternative New Year's Day** event, His new book, **There Are Too Many Words In My House**, will appear in 2018 from **Poets Wear Prada**.

———————

Francine Witte is the author of five chapbooks. Her full-length poetry collection, Caf Crazy, is forthcoming from Kelsay Books. She lives in NYC.

———————

Jeffrey Cyphers Wright is the author of 15 books of verse, including most recently **Blue Lyre** from **Dos Madres Press**, **Radio Poems** from **The Operating System** and **Party Everywhere** from **Xanadu**. New work is included in **New American Writing**, 2017. Wright edits **Live Mag! www.livemag.org / www.jeffreycypherswright. com**

Alphabetical Index Of Poems

•

ROGUE SCHOLARS
Press

For General Information, go to:

http://www.alternativenyd.org

For more information or a price quote for our
book design and editing services, contact:

editor@roguescholars.com

•

Other ANYDSWPE Volumes:

Forever Night (Siempre Noche) - 2017
Rogue Scholars Press
ISBN-13: 978-0-9840982-4-8

Palabras Luminosas (Luminous Words) - 2016
Rogue Scholars Press
ISBN-13: 978-0-9840982-3-1

Shadow Of The Geode (Sombra Del Geode) - 2015
Bonsai Publishers
ISBN-13: 978-1-9424630-0-9 (1st Edition)

Estrellas En El Fuego (Stars In The Fire) - 2014
Rogue Scholars Press
ISBN-13: 978-0-9840982-9-3

•

24 Years!

**The Alternative New Year's Day
Spoken Word / Performance Extravaganza**

http://AlternativeNYD.org

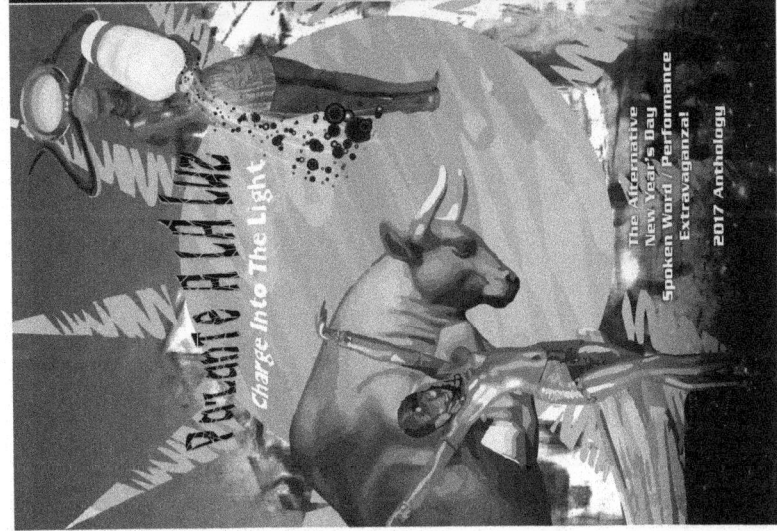

Palabras Luninosas

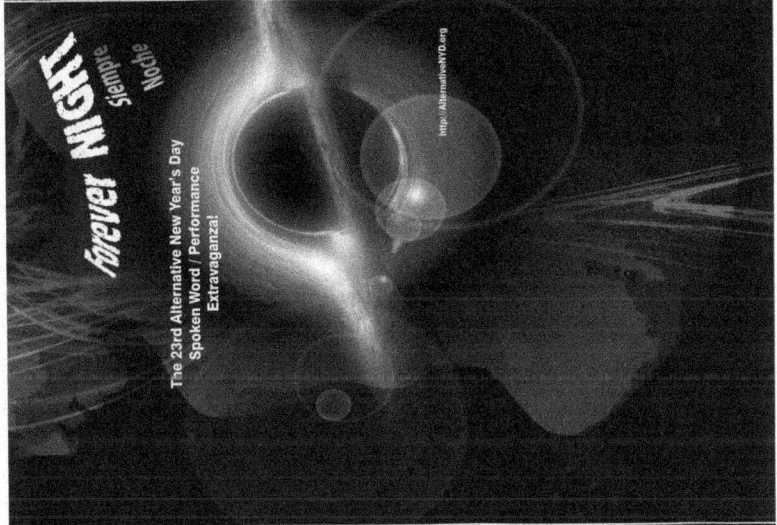

Forever Night

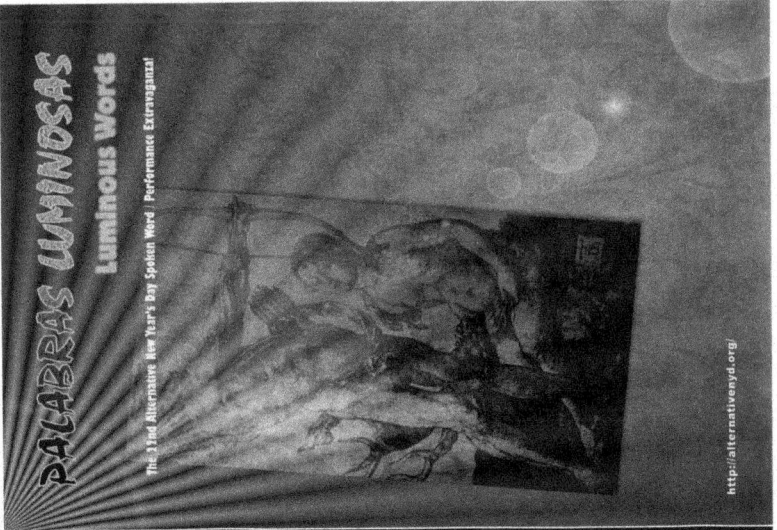

Pa'lante A La Luz

Shadow Of The Geode

Estrellas En El Fuego

Black Blizzard

Broken Light

www.SpokenWordExtravaganza.org

Dark Matters

www.SpokenWordExtravaganza.org

Kaleidoscope

www.SpokenWordExtravaganza.org

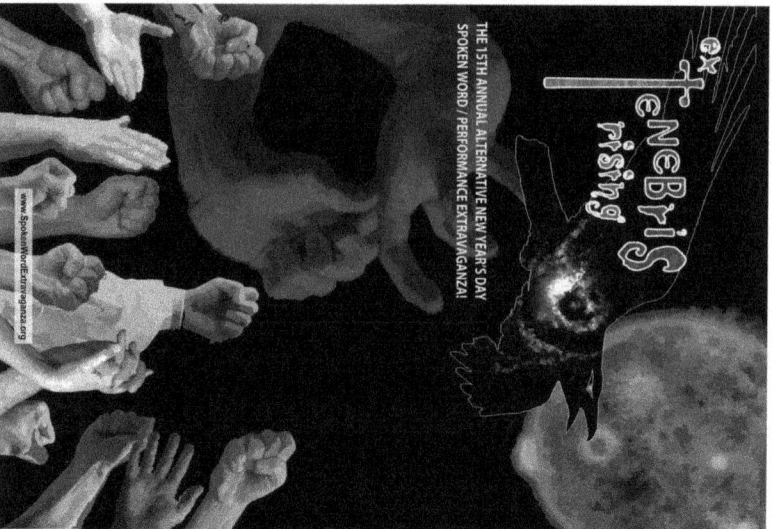

Ex Tenebris

ex Tenebris rising

THE 15TH ANNUAL ALTERNATIVE NEW YEAR'S DAY
SPOKEN WORD / PERFORMANCE EXTRAVAGANZA!

www.SpokenWordExtravaganza.org

Futurus Lux

FUTURUS LUX
Light Of The Future

The 14th Annual Alternative
New Year's Day Spoken Word /
Performance Extravaganza

www.SpokenWordExtravaganza.org

Event Horizon

EVENT HORIZON
The 13th Annual New Year's Day
Spoken Word / Performance Extravaganza

www.AlternativeSpokenWord.com